PUMP AND CIRCUMSTANCE

FULL
SERVICE
NO SMOKING
STOP ENGINES
REGULAR
UNLEADED

JOHN MARGOLIES

PUMP AND CIRCUMSTANCE

GLORY DAYS OF THE GAS STATION

A Bulfinch Press Book
Little, Brown and Company
Boston • New York • Toronto • London

Frontispiece: Conoco station, Arlington, Kansas

Title page: Johnson's Magnolia Service Station, Houston, Texas

First Paperback Edition, 1996

Some of the illustrations in this book are published with the permission of private collectors, institutions, and corporations who are listed with the illustration credits on page 126.

Margolies, John.
Pump and circumstance : the glory days of the gas station / John Margolies. — 1st ed.
p. cm.
Includes bibliographical references.
ISBN 0-8212-1995-2 (hardcover)
ISBN 0-8212-2284-8 (paperback)
1. Service stations—United States — History. I. Title.
TL 153.M36 1993
629.28'6'0973 — dc20

Bulfinch Press is an imprint and trademark of Little, Brown and Company (Inc.). Published simultaneously in Canada by Little, Brown & Company (Canada) Limited

Design by Eric Baker Design Associates, Inc.

Printed In Singapore

CONTENTS

CHAPTER 1

PUMP AND CIRCUMSTANCE

Problem number one: How to get gasoline into the tank of a car? At the turn of the century, some motorists would get a large oil drumful from an industrial depot, bring it home, and store it someplace. Often these barrels had a spigot at the bottom; the gasoline was transferred to a spouted can, and then poured through a chamois filter into the tank. This entire process was smelly, time-consuming, and *dangerous*.

Comic advertisement from a 1914 Bowser Company manual.

The first retail outlets for gas were blacksmith shops and hardware and grocery stores, the same places where kerosene was bought to burn in lamps. The same process of getting the gas into the tank prevailed, with the safer alternative of not storing the fuel at home offset by the bother of having to go someplace else to get it. Sometimes gas was sold from a barrel on wheels brought to the car, while horse-drawn tanks could make house calls.

The first "gas station" of the Gilmore Oil Company, Los Angeles, was a horse-drawn tank in the early 1900s.

SOME DAY YOU WILL OWN
A HORSELESS CARRIAGE
OUR GASOLINE WILL RUN IT. GILMORE OIL CO.

A woman and her faithful friend pose beside a tall gas pump in Lyndhurst, New Jersey, in this 1936 hand-tinted photograph.

This metal sign, circa 1920, was painted in ten colors by the Stanford Crowell Company, Ithaca, New York.

At the top of its "filling station" cabinets, the Bowser Pump Company custom-painted the doors to the pump with the logos of specific major highways.

What to do to make this simpler? American ingenuity and the Industrial Revolution to the rescue. In 1885, in his barn in Fort Wayne, Indiana, Sylvanus F. Bowser came up with the idea of a water pump in which a wooden plunger would raise a column of water upward to the surface. Bowser devised "a self-measuring gasoline tank" for $10, which delivered coal oil from a barrel. Bowser's first customer, one Jake Gumper, was a grocer who sold stove gas. Soon thereafter, Gumper quit his business and went to work for Bowser.

As gasoline, formerly a useless by-product of the refining process, became a necessity, the Bowser pump was adapted to pump gas from a fifty-gallon container permanently installed outside in a wooden cabinet. In 1905, Mr. Gumper described this apparatus as a "filling station" and painted these words in bold lettering on the outside of the cabinet. And thus the first predecessor of a curbside pump was born. Or, perhaps, this was the first gas station, but more about that later.

There were four major gas pump producers and dozens of smaller pump companies (at least one hundred is a good, educated guess) that sprang up, almost by spontaneous combustion, in the teens and twenties, each with its own special gimmick or gadget. As one befuddled gas pump authority stated in 1942: "The almost infinite variety of models and designs of gasoline pumps produced in the past third of a century beggar description."

Gasoline storage was safer in underground tanks as illustrated in a 1915 Bowser Company manual.

Curbside pumps, usually in dense downtown locations, became a very common way to get gas, but they had their disadvantages: street traffic became congested by lines of people waiting to get gas; and it was hazardous to locate a pump right beside the road. A car could swerve and easily bash into a pump, and then all hell might break loose. Local ordinances were passed to prevent these curbside outlets from proliferating any further, leading to the next important step — getting the pumps back off the street.

In 1907, John McLean opened a "drive-through" station in Seattle for Standard Oil of California. Inside a little building off the street, McLean rigged up a tank on a platform with a glass measuring device and a hose. The motorist drove in one side, got a tankful, and drove out the other side.

A number of minor advances contributed to the state of the art: in 1902, the first underground tanks; in 1904, a full-stroke delivery device, one (and then five) gallon per stroke; by 1910, a sight glass with spinners and an audible bell (one clang per gallon) were added, giving an aura of drama to the otherwise mundane experience; and by 1912, an electrically lighted globe was added atop the pump just for advertising (floodlights to illuminate the entire pump area didn't come along until 1923).

A twin-cylinder visible pump dwarfs a Canadian metroplis in this 1934 Imperial Oil illustration by A. J. Casson.

A real-photo postcard shows an unusual double-cylinder visible pump manufactured in the 1920s.

Visible pump, Centreville, Alabama.

Visible pump, Winnemucca, Nevada.

All of these early devices were known as "blind pumps" because the consumer could not see the product as it was being purchased, and this led to suspicion and mistrust by motorists. This problem was allayed by the next great advance in gas pump design — the introduction of the visible or gravity pump in the late teens. These huge (ten to eleven feet high) anthropomorphic creations featured a five- or ten-gallon glass cylinder on the upper extremities, with ladder-like measuring indicators mounted inside. The gas was hand-pumped into these cylinders, and then gravity-fed into the tank. Since the consumers could now see the product they were buying, gas companies began to dye the gasoline to establish product identity — Texaco was green, Esso was red, and Sunoco was blue. Legend has it that the shade of blue used for Sunoco matched the color of a tile chip from the roof of China's Temple of Heaven (the chip given to Sun Oil chairman Joseph N. Pew and his wife while on their honeymoon in China in 1916).

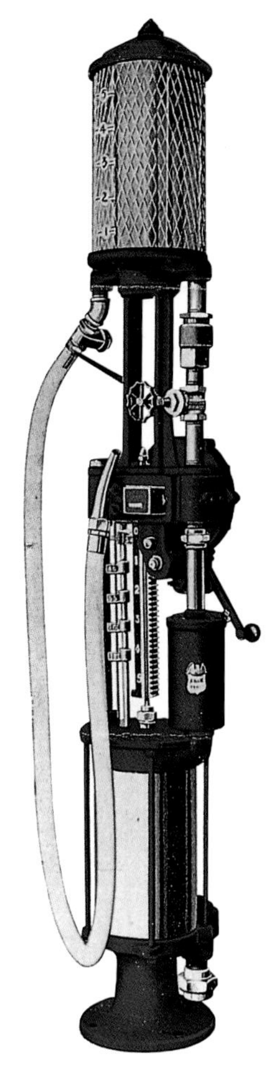

A brochure view of an American Brand visible pump with a five-gallon cylinder.

Nevada roadside entrepreneur "Dad Lee" poses beside a Tokheim visible pump at his Shell station in this 1930s real-photo postcard.

The visible pump was enormously popular in the 1920s, although one peculiar flaw endemic to this device became quite obvious — as the sun shone upon the gasoline in the cylinder, it caused a disgusting brown film to form. The pump companies, along with the Corning Glass Works, saved the day by perfecting "Nultra," a blue-tinted glass that blocked out ultraviolet rays and prevented the unwanted scum.

Two more major problems needed to be solved before the gas pump as we know it today came into being. The manual pumping mechanism had to be replaced with a more convenient process, and a way had to be invented to compute and measure each sale. By 1923, the first problem was solved when an electric motor-driven visible pump was introduced. In 1929, the second problem was solved with the introduction of the first metered pump. These "thinking pumps" measured both the amount of gasoline (including fractions of gallons) and also the precise price (including tenths of cents) simultaneously.

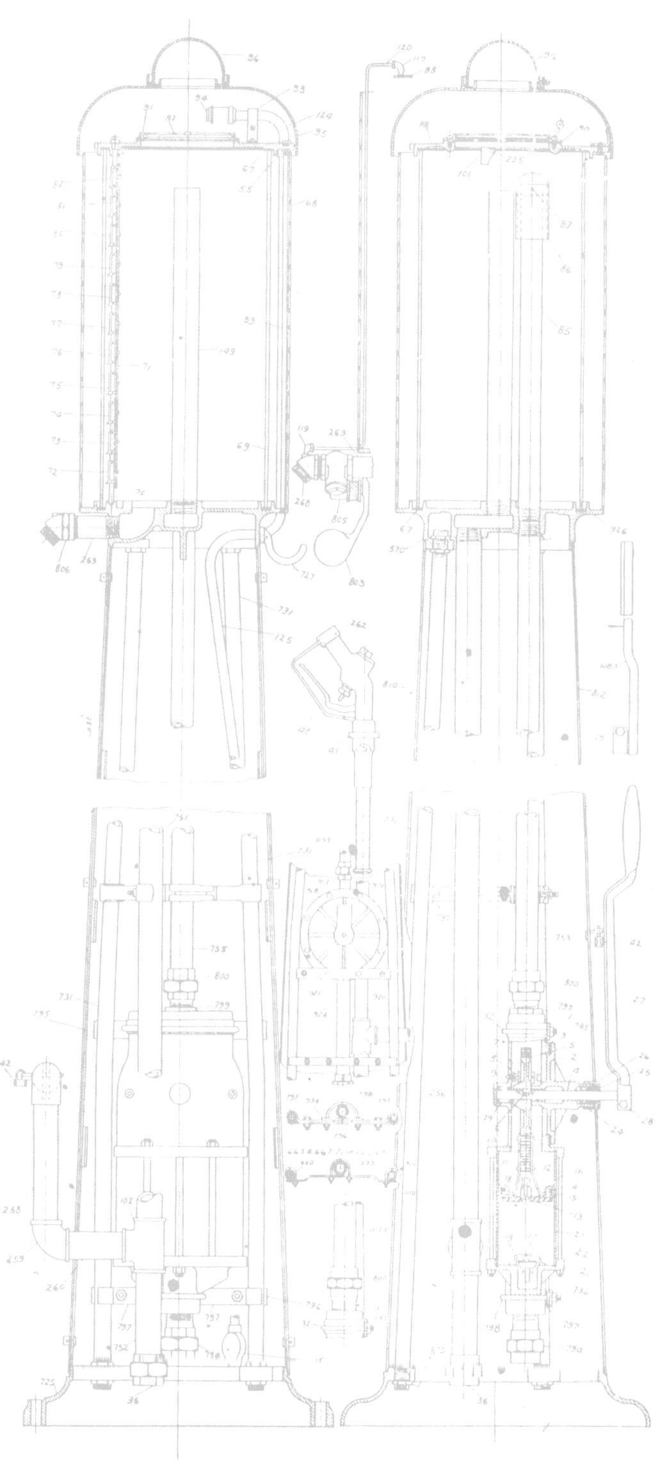

Instruction manual drawings, 1928, for the Wayne Company visible pump, the most common and popular of this genre.

A trio of Texaco-globed calculating pumps, Milford, Illinois.

The first calculating pumps were still quite tall in stature, and they had "clockface" gauges, with the small "hour" hand pointing to the gallons dispensed and the larger "minute" hand pointing to fractions of gallons, and all of this accompanied by a sight glass through which the motorist could view the gas as it went into the tank. Then the familiar spinning dials came along with a hypnotic visible gauge and spinner on the pump face.

A 1942 advertisement in the *Saturday Evening Post* for the "Honest Measure" of Wayne calculating pumps was based upon the almost unbelievable premise that a retail consumer would buy gas based upon the manufacturer of the pump. An immaculately clad, coiffed, and accessorized woman is shown answering the compelling question stated in the headline:

"Do I pay attention to gas pumps?"

"YES, FRANKLY, I DO," she says.

The ad copy goes on to have the woman explain to us: "I'm just as thrifty in buying gasoline as I am in buying potatoes or clothes for the children. . . . I wouldn't know one pump from another, but I've read the advertisements that say these Wayne Pumps can't make a mistake . . . so I look for them every time. Feminine or not — it's sound reasoning."

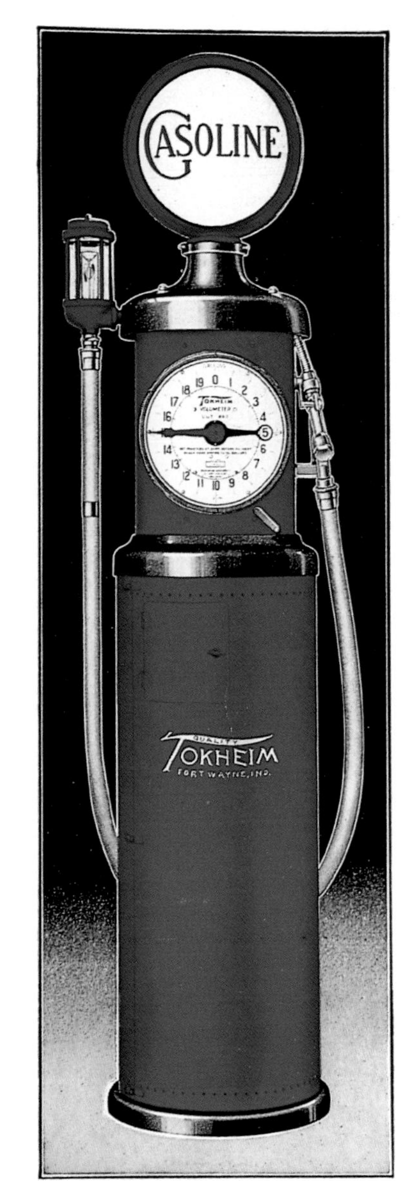

Tokheim clockface pump blotter from the 1930s.

An old Atlantic White Flash clockface pump, above, clings to life in Hawley, Pennsylvania, while a Wayne calculating pump, right, in the prime of its life, is dramatically portrayed by Steven Dohanos in this 1937 illustration for *Fortune* magazine.

The calculating pumps of the 1930s had all of the elements of present-day pumps, and over the next fifty years various design refinements were made. Minor advances included nozzle shutoff, zero setback, self-retracting hoses, dual or tandem pumps, and "multi-blending pumps which permitted several grades of gasoline to be sold from the same pump." After World War II the pumps began to shrink in stature. The new "eye-level" or lo-boy models got smaller when the pumping mechanism, formerly located in the cabinet aboveground, was placed belowground.

Sunoco figural matchbook from the 1940s.

A matched pair of More gas pumps, Nephi, Utah.

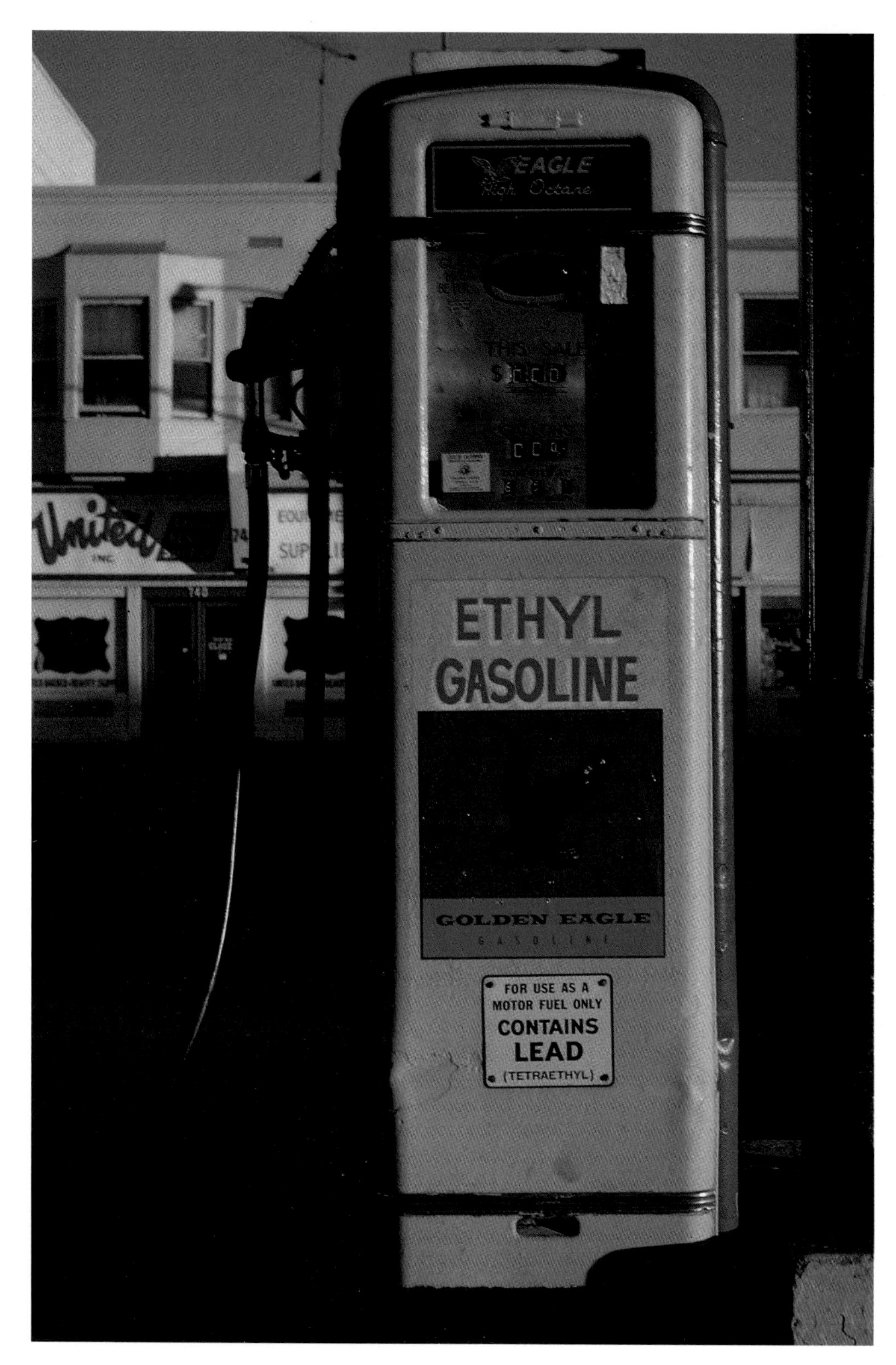

Golden Eagle Gas Pump, San Diego, California.

In this hand-tinted and airbrushed photograph, circa 1940, a visionary transformed an Atlantic station into part of the gas pumps. The dispensing units are out front, as usual, but the gas pump gauges are located in the arched form on top of the station.

By the 1970s nearly all the drama was gone at the new self-service digital computer pump islands connected to central controls. And, by the 1980s, the difficult-to-operate, but environmentally friendly, vapor recovery pump nozzles were introduced.

Within a century, jerry-built and hazardous devices have evolved into sophisticated and technologically advanced equipment. But, as with nearly everything else, as the technology was perfected, the gas pump, as an object, lost its heart and soul. The tall and almost superhuman-looking pumps of days gone by, with intricate and specialized profiles, have been replaced by sleek, small, totally efficient vending machines.

This enormous mural is located in the first-floor conference room of the corporate headquarters of Marathon Oil in Findlay, Ohio. It was painted by artists Andrew Karoly and Louis Szanto in the 1950s, and depicts the history and heroic deeds of the workers in the oil industry.

CIRCUMSTANCE

Before there was a gas pump, there had to be oil. Crude oil and natural gas had been around for millions of years, and some of it bubbled to the surface of the earth as natural deposits. The great moment in oil exploration in the United States came in 1859, when a man named Edwin Drake drilled and struck oil along the Oil Creek in the Venango Valley at Titusville in western Pennsylvania.

Colonel Drake's great discovery started a frenzy of activity not seen since the California gold rush of a decade earlier. The "black gold" rush of the late nineteenth and early twentieth centuries was a full-blown saga fueled by tales and myths of rags to riches, boom and bust, and gushers and dry holes. John D. Rockefeller, a twenty-three-year-old businessman from Cleveland, made his first oil investment in 1863, and started the Standard Oil Company in the late 1860s. Standard Oil grew into a monopolistic trust and controlled nearly every aspect of oil production until 1909, when a court, enforcing the Sherman Antitrust Act of 1890, carved up the trust into little pieces.

The big moment for independent oil producers in America came in 1901 with the discovery of an enormous gusher at the Spindletop oil field near Beaumont, Texas, giving the United States the title of the world's largest oil producer, a position it held on to for nearly fifty years.

Why was there so much commotion about crude oil? It certainly wasn't about gasoline. Before the automobile, nobody knew what to do with it, and so it was thrown away. Everyone was after kerosene, a virtually smokeless and odorless illuminant to burn

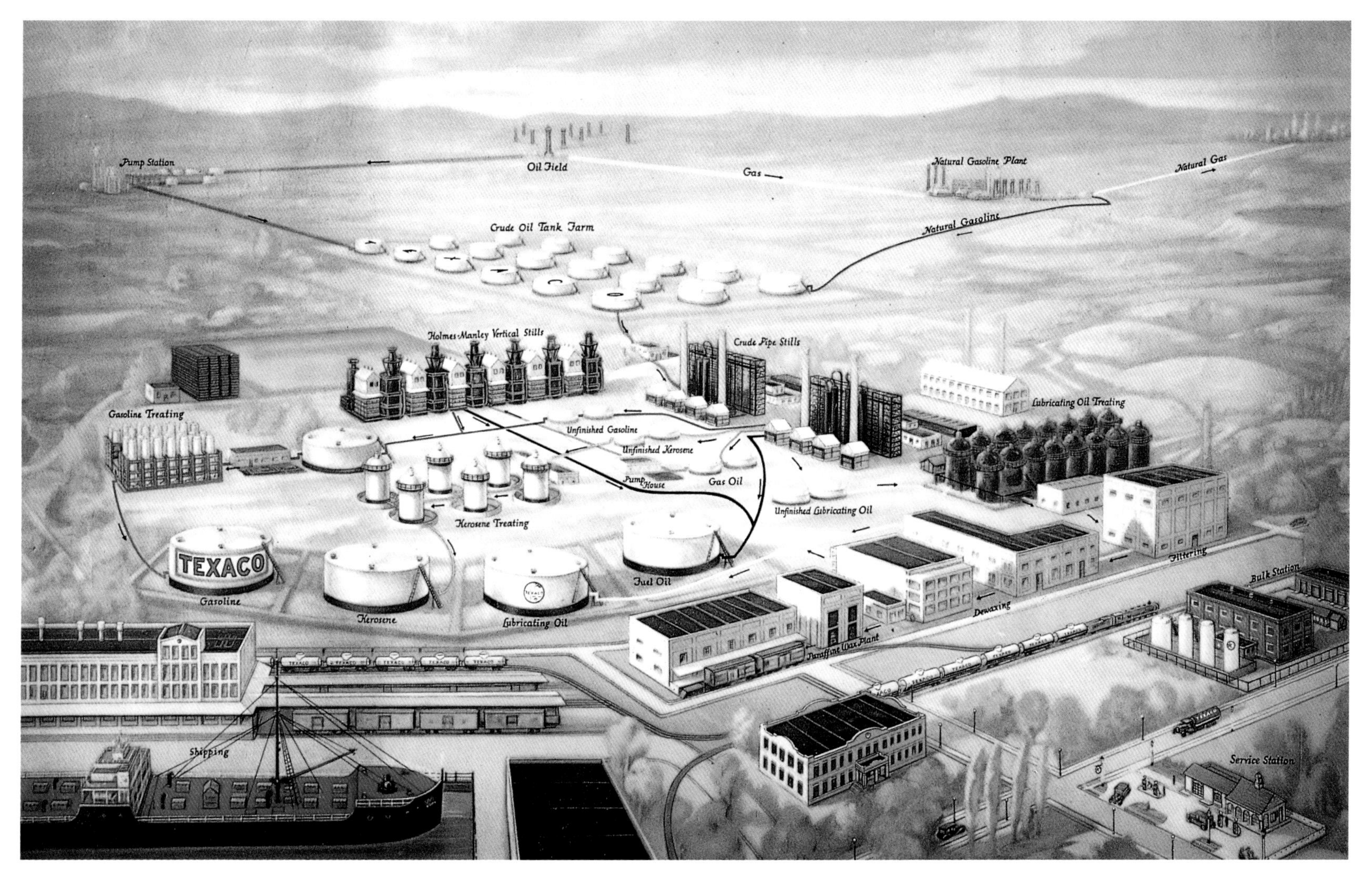

In the elaborate promotional illustration, "Petroleum And Its Products From Well To Market," issued by Texaco in the 1930s, a cute little neighborhood gas station, depicted in the lower right corner, is just the tip of a huge corporate iceberg.

in lamps, superior to whale oil and coal oil because it didn't flicker.

In the early twentieth century, as the oil boom was becoming a glut, the missing links — cars and roads — needed to complete the phenomenon of delirious self-mobility in the United States were simultaneously being developed. J. Charles and Frank Duryea perfected a gasoline engine motor car in 1892 or '93, and others were hard at work soon after. By 1898 there were some 800 cars in the United States, and this number grew to 8,000 by 1900.

In 1903, Henry Ford founded his company, stating, "I will make a motor car for the multitude." Ford's Model T cost $850 in 1908, and more than 19,000 were sold in 1909. By 1913 Ford was mass-producing 1,000 cars a day, and the price kept dropping until a Model T cost only $290 by 1924.

Roads, a motorist's nightmare, began to improve quickly. The bicycle craze in the late nineteenth century had given birth to a "better roads" movement, and by 1904 there were already 200,000 miles of paved road. Roads got better as the oil asphalt, a gooey remnant of the refining process, was used for paving.

In this dramatic photograph from 1925, left, a Phillips 66 gusher erupts from one well in the Burbank field of northeastern Oklahoma, while business appears to be brisk at this oil field, above, depicted in this1950 West Canadian Oil & Gas Limited stock certificate illustration.

"Motoring" had become transportation by 1910, and the face of America had changed forever. No longer constricted by the narrow tracks and routes of railroads, the American tourism industry was born, and millions of adventurers set out to explore the United States and fulfill their destiny.

Suddenly, gasoline was very much in demand, and the production of gasoline surpassed that of kerosene for the first time in 1909. The world would never be the same.

Gas attendant statue, Clarksville, Arkansas.

The "highest stack of empty oil cans in the world," 50 feet high and 20 feet wide, was the 1930s inspiration of Max Taubert , who wanted to make sure that motorists would take notice on old Route 10. Now the station has been bypassed and Mr. Taubert died long ago, but his renowned monument still stands as a cherished local landmark.

SIGNS

In addition to their products, the single most important asset for an oil company is its graphic symbol and logo. Drawing upon nearly every sort of imagery imaginable, companies made quirky and idiosyncratic decisions about how to present themselves to the public. The gasoline dispensed from one brand's pump wasn't all that different from another's.

This huge oil can sign once stood near Hollywood, California.

A glorious tower of tires denoted a gas station in Los Angeles in the 1920s.

Long before motorists even see a gas station, they see a sign. It is hung out front perpendicular to the road to proclaim itself as loudly as possible. The older signs, sometimes made of wood, painted metal, or, later, baked porcelain enamel on steel, were designed to appeal to people going more slowly. Therefore, many content-laden, representational symbols were used. Their finer articulation could be at least discerned by the passing motorist.

An enormous tower-sign near Mount Shasta, California, not only proclaimed a Richfield gas station to automobiles, but also served as part of an airplane navigation system built by Richfield along the West Coast from the Mexican to the Canadian borders.

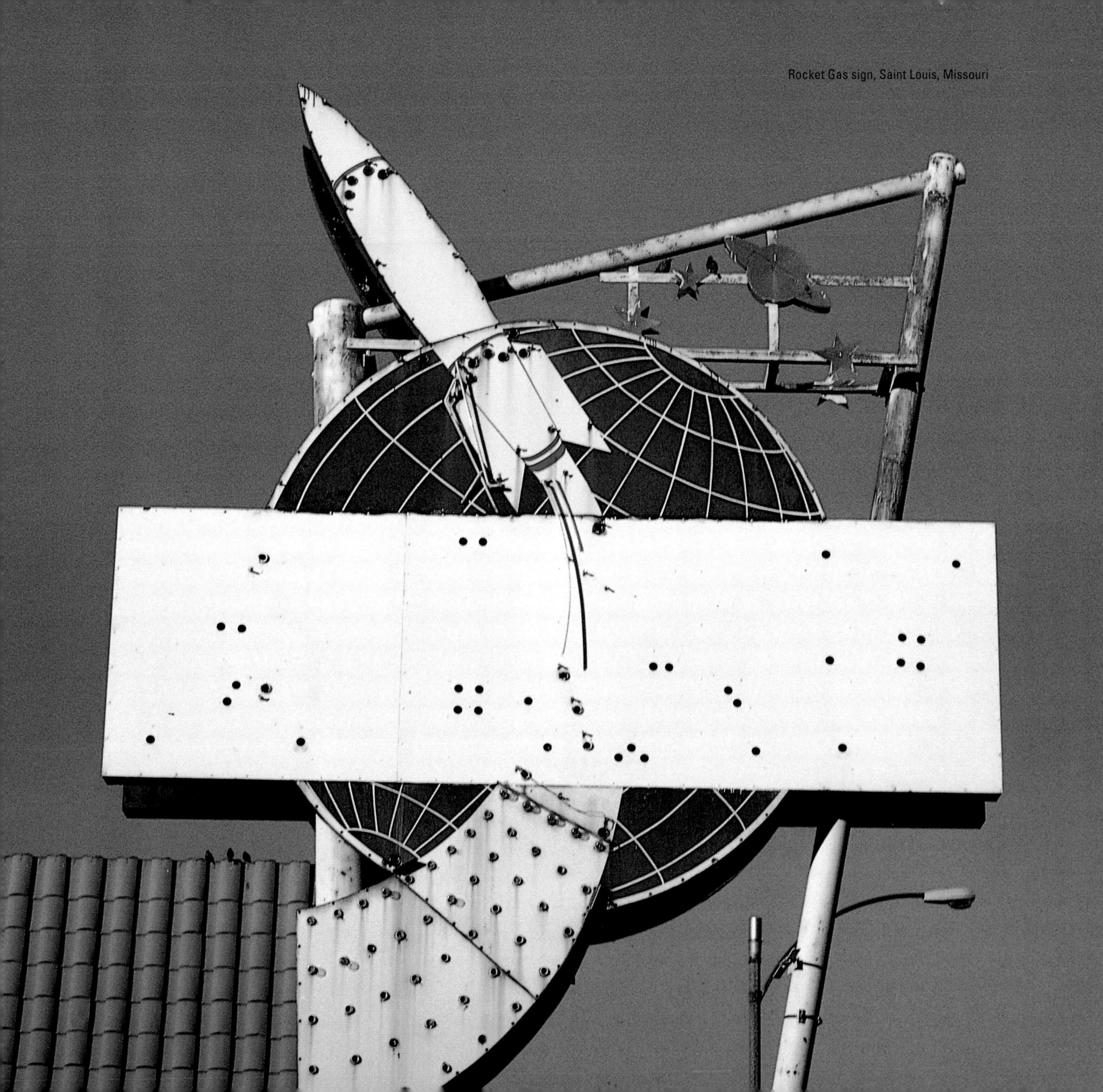

Rocket Gas sign, Saint Louis, Missouri

Litening Gas decal.

Selma, Alabama.

Dighton, Massachusetts.

Boise, Idaho.

SIGNS

Graphic design changed to serve the new needs created by the interstate highway system. Now people were driving at 60 or 70 miles per hour on roads with restricted rights-of-way and limited access. The new signs were larger and simplified. The folksy apparitions of yesteryear were replaced by depictions of subject matter like a corporation's initials.

Like nearly everything else in the gas station business, the old seems somehow better than the new. We have the advantage of 100 percent clear hindsight to savor and enjoy what isn't there anymore. But it's very hard to become attached to today's "contemporary" graphic images.

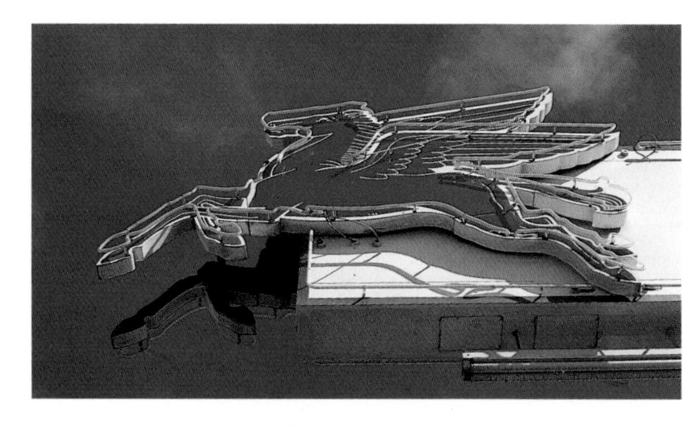
Gallup, New Mexico.

Selma, Alabama.

Muskegon, Michigan.

Chickasha, Oklahoma.

Ann Sheridan for Signal Gasoline decal.

Native State Gasoline decal.

Florence, Colorado.

Muskegon, Michigan.

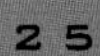

CHAPTER 2

PIONEER DAYS

The Bowser Pump Company's cabinet door design for the National Old Trails Road was a tour de force in its graphic design and its execution, circa 1915.

Just where and when the first gas station appeared is a matter of considerable conjecture. Much like trying to determine who came up with the first ice-cream cone or the first hamburger, the answer is shrouded in tall tales and folklore. There is certainly no definitive answer to this "first" question.

We do know for sure that no one really knew how to design a gas station because there had never been one before. And the first generation of gas pumps as we now know them didn't come along until about 1910. So the first dispensing outlets, "filling stations" not "service stations" (various "services" didn't evolve until later on, and repairs were taken care of at garages and blacksmith shops), were makeshift creations involving a tank and a hose, usually at curbside, sometimes in or near a little building.

There may have been "the first public station" for storing and dispensing gasoline in 1901 in New York City, and a chain in Boston later that year. But that's as detailed as these "first" claims get.

Looking a little like a catastrophe just waiting to happen, the "first filling station in Findlay, Ohio, which opened in 1913, sold Standard Oil's Red Crown gasoline."

GHASTER POSTER ADV. CO.
Lockhart's
MILL·END·SALE
The Economy Event of the Year
Monday AUG. 28 THRU Saturday SEPT. 9
MIL·NER'S-Toled
WILL YOU BE THERE?
Old Man Mileage recommends
REPUBLIC
Mileage TIRES
ELECTRIC CONST. & MOTOR CO.
23.
RED CROWN GASOLINE
AUTO
FILLING STATION
RED CROWN GASOLINE
ZEROLENE
MATCHLESS LIQUID GLOSS
DAYTON AIRLESS TIRES
RED CROWN GASOLINE
Polarine
FAIR

Ansel Adams would have liked to fill up at this gas station in Yosemite National Park, circa 1920.

Then, there were several other "first" stations. The Oriental Oil Company had a "pumping stand" with a pump in a building at curbside, the pipe going under the sidewalk to a tank, in Dallas in 1903. By 1905, the American Gasoline Company of Saint Louis had a "drive-in" station on a corner lot.

By 1913, "first" accounts were becoming more detailed and convincing. Standard Oil of Ohio built a drive-through station in Columbus which opened in 1913. It was a 20x14-foot prefabricated metal building erected overnight (to circumvent possible neighborhood objections). A car would enter from one end,

An elaborate Greek-inspired temple of petroleum, sheathed in glazed terra-cotta tile, was built by the Atlantic Refining Company in Philadelphia about 1916.

and on one side there were two pumps. On the other side were shelves containing automotive products. With a full tank, the motorist would exit through the opposite end.

A drive-up service station opened by the Gulf Oil Corporation at the intersection of Baum Boulevard and St. Clair Street in Pittsburgh, in 1913, seems to be the real forerunner of the more sophisticated outlets which were soon to evolve across the United States. It was a hexagonal masonry building with roof overhangs on all sides. Gas pumps were deployed around the building, accessible by concrete driveways from both streets. Invitations were sent to potential customers in the area, and on the first day of operation, December 1, 1913, some 30 gallons of gas were sold. By the first Saturday the gallon count was up to 350. The station offered "free" crankcase service and would also fill radiators and inflate tires.

Two attendants pose proudly at this 1914 Standard Oil of Kentucky station in Winchester, Kentucky.

Many of the early gas stations were eyesores and a blight to their communities—ugly little buildings that were dangerous and generated unwanted noise. Oil companies realized these shortcomings, and by the midteens they were building less offensive gas stations, not only for public-spirited reasons, but for purposes of product identification and advertising. Since all across America petroleum companies were selling, essentially or actually, the very same product, the gas station itself was the definitive physical manifestation of each brand's identity.

Many oil companies had standardized, functional designs that they spread across the landscape of their territories. Standard Oil of Ohio perfected its "Type A" station by the midteens—a little shed with a hip roof with pumps located beneath a canopy supported by a single, decorative column.

Standard Oil of California developed its own standard model, which cost from $500 to $1,500 to build; these stations were made more attractive with lawns and flower gardens.

"Look...they gave me a map!" an excited motorist is exclaiming to his companion in this 1934 Gulf magazine advertisement celebrating the twentieth anniversary of Gulf's giving away the first free road map in 1914. Although there are no known surviving copies of this first map, the map cover shown above, from 1916, is nearly identical.

In World War I, Standard Oil of California replaced the flower gardens at its stations with model vegetable gardens "to solve the problem of feeding the nations."

Die-cut booklet cover for Xerolene Motor Oil, 1917.

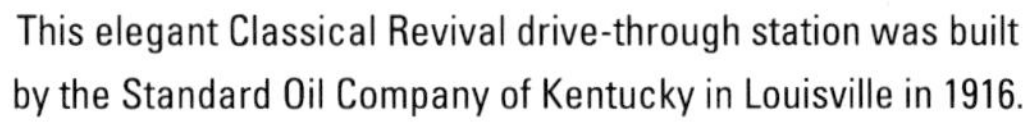
This elegant Classical Revival drive-through station was built by the Standard Oil Company of Kentucky in Louisville in 1916.

The number of gas stations grew slowly but surely throughout the United States in the decade of the teens. Although no specific statistics were recorded in this era, there were probably not more than a few thousand stations, although they were said to be growing in number by some 1,200 a year. Filling stations were far outnumbered by the 18,000 garages selling gas by 1920.

A gleaming, majestic dome highlights the design of this station in Dallas, Texas.

The trend toward station beautification continued in the late teens. An early Vacuum Oil Company publication proclaimed that gas stations "should be an ornament to the community rather than a blight on the landscape." The *National Petroleum News* held an annual competition with a prize of $100 for the most attractive gas station.

One wave of the future, the building of elaborate and spectacular gas stations, began in 1915 when the Atlantic Refining Company opened its opulent outlet in Pittsburgh. This station, the first in a series of Atlantic extravaganzas, was a miniature temple in high Greek Revival style. It had very proper and well-proportioned Greek columns and capitals, and it was sheathed in gleaming white glazed terra-cotta tile with colored accents and trim.

Wadhams Service Station—N. 27 St. and W. Wisconsin Ave., Milwaukee, Wisconsin

Other companies were soon to follow Atlantic's high-minded approach. The Wadhams Oil Company in Milwaukee commissioned an architect to come up with a station design that would be easily distinguishable and that would display the company colors—red, yellow, and black. Architect Alexander C. Eschweiler outdid himself in choosing an exotic and romantic design motif, and in 1917, the first Wadhams gas station, said to look like a Japanese tea house, opened its doors. Its dominant feature was an elaborate pagoda-like roof covered with bright red stamped metal tiles, and eight-inch-thick brick walls painted yellow. Very soon, neighborhoods throughout Milwaukee had their very own Japanese shrines of petroleum.

The Atlantic and Wadhams stations were the beginning of a new wave of architectural splendor in the stations soon to come along in the 1920s and 1930s. The glory days of the gas station were beginning. The roadside was being embellished by imaginative and distinctive, one-of-a-kind solutions to a new universal design problem in America.

Beginning in 1917, the Wadhams Oil Company in Milwaukee, Wisconsin, built an elaborate series of stations said to look like "Japanese tea houses." Perhaps the most elaborate example, seen in a postcard view, left, had an intricate, multilevel pagoda roof. One survivor, belonging to Harley Sprague, became a local Milwaukee landmark.

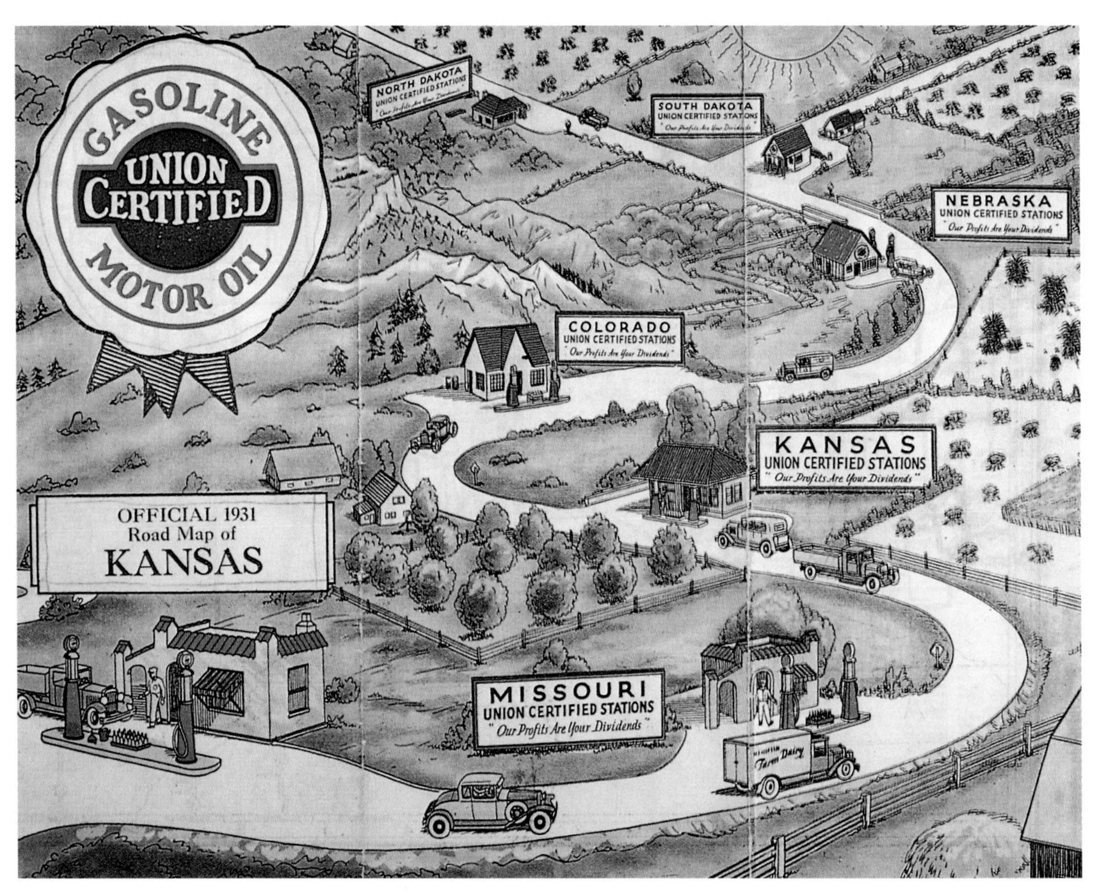

Although this map for the small Union Certified Gas Company dates from 1931, it still has the line drawing quality of maps produced earlier in the 1920s.

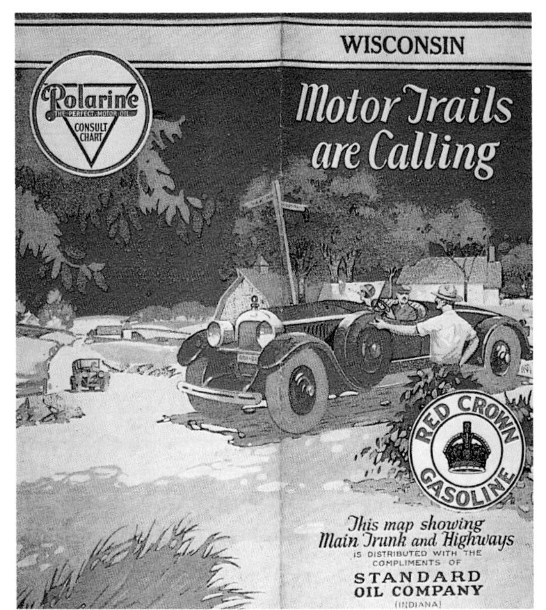

ROAD MAPS

The road map is surely the most significant artifact of the automotive age. It is every bit as important a symbol of the new mobility as the freedom of movement itself. Given out by the oil companies as the ultimate piece of advertising to promote the use of their products, the maps charted the yellow brick roads of our collective imagination.

Experts generally agree that the Gulf Oil Company gave away the first free road maps in Pittsburgh in 1914. The map was 12 by 10 inches, with a roadster depicted on the cover. By 1914, Gulf had given out 300,000 state maps, and by 1920 it had distributed some 16,000,000 state maps.

But these road maps were even more than tickets to paradise. Walter W. Ristow, an eminent historian of cartography at the Library of Congress, in a definitive article marking the fiftieth anniversary of the phenomenon in 1964, stated: "These useful maps ... are among the distinctive and essential by-products of our modern automobile culture. They are a uniquely American contribution to the development of cartography."

Standard Oil of Indiana issued this road map cover of a rural scene in 1924. The subject matter is charming, with a farmer giving directions to a couple driving what must have been one of the largest roadsters anywhere, but the color range of red, blue, and little else is still limited.

This rather primitive road map of Ontario and Quebec, circa 1924, is the earliest known Canadian oil company example.

In 1931 the Standard Oil Company of California issued a road map cover about road maps as a flapper type looks up from rather than at the map in her hands.

Road map covers from the early 1920s, like this Alabama map from Standard Oil of Kentucky, predated the use of elaborate printing techniques and emphasized finely detailed line drawings and a limited palette of colors.

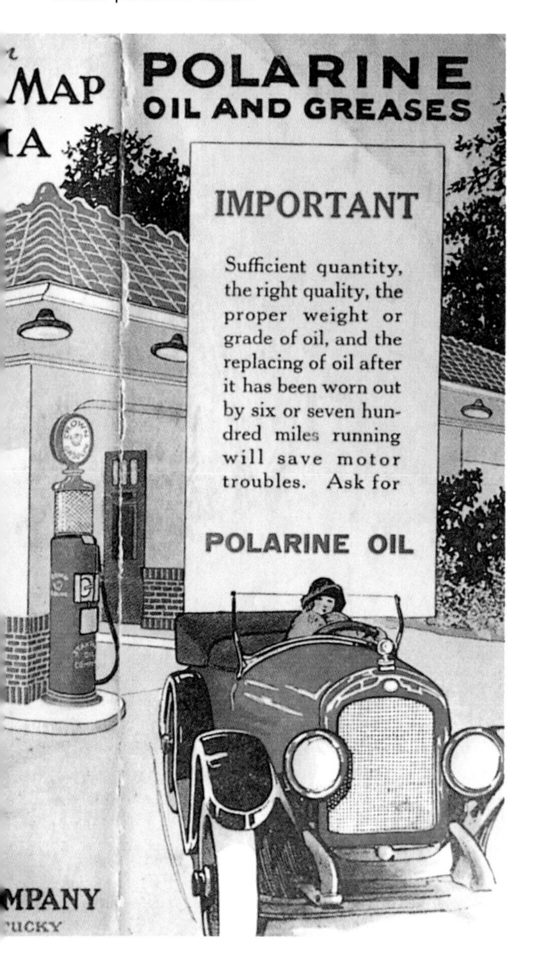

The earliest road map far predates Gulf's first free handout. In 1895 the *Chicago Times Herald* issued the "first" road map as it sponsored a 54-mile automobile race from Chicago to Waukegan and back. There were also route maps for bicycle enthusiasts at this time, but these weren't of much use to motorists who needed wider thoroughfares.

The Automobile Club of America was organized in 1899, and they issued their first "Blue Book" in 1901, which contained maps as well as verbal directional instructions. The Blue Books and other early road guides were cumbersome and inefficient, especially as roads improved and multiplied, and speed limits increased.

From 1905 to 1910 there were photo maps being published as well, with small maps and photographs of important intersections and guideposts. The Rand McNally Company, which began in 1868 in Chicago by printing railroad tickets, guides, and timetables, had issued its first road map by 1904, and also began to produce photo maps.

The second major player in the road map business was the General Drafting Company, founded in New York City in 1909 by an immigrant from Finland, Otto G. Lindberg, and which issued its first product in 1912, a state map of Vermont. The third of the big three in road maps, the J. M. Gousha Company, didn't come along until much later, in 1926, and was founded by former Rand McNally employees.

In any discussion of early road maps, it is important to realize that prior to 1918, when Wisconsin became the first state to number its roads, routes were unmarked. And a coordinated federal numbering system wasn't adopted until 1926.

By 1927, Standard Oil of Kentucky has abandoned their earlier, more conservative covers in favor of dazzling and brilliant landscapes depicted beside their stations.

The Mona Motor Gasoline Company in 1930 employed fanciful comic book–like drawings and brilliant coloration to tell everyone about their gas stations and their radio station.

As seen in this spectacular road map issued by Conoco, oil companies spared no expense in utilizing the most sophisticated color printing techniques to produce maps that customers would be proud to store in their glove compartments.

In the 1930s the Richfield Oil Company of California issued booklets of strip maps to give away to consumers. Throughout the decade, each new booklet cover seemed to outdo the previous year's spectacular graphic design. The 1934 cover of a little gas station in the redwoods is almost surreal and Magritte-like, except there is no quirky anomaly disturbing the overall perfection of the idealized image. The 1937 cover is commercial art of the highest order, with its Futurist-Fauve demeanor almost bordering on abstraction.

The Rio Grande Petroleum Company, by 1939 a subsidiary of Richfield Oil, celebrates the heritage of California in this map booklet cover depicting a Spanish dancer.

The 1933 Phillips 66 "bathing suit" map of Missouri is both sensational and riveting. Using a limited palette of colors, Phillips shows us a woman in a high-style swimming suit waving at us beside a lake shore scene.

ROAD MAPS

In 1916, Rand McNally offered a $100 prize to the employee who came up with the best new map product idea. The winner was John G. Brink, who suggested that the company name and mark with signs the major American highways — an activity that the company came to call "blazing trails." So Brink and his associates headed out and nailed up unique graphic symbols for the roads, a pyramid sign for "The Egyptian Trail" being just one example. By 1920, Rand McNally had blazed 50,000 miles of roads accompanied by "Auto Trails Maps," and by 1922, it had covered all of the states and had the first series of road maps issued coast to coast.

The General Drafting Company made its own significant contribution to the art of road mapping. In 1920, in a map it produced for the First National Bank of Boston, it began to classify roads by type and condition. And as the cartography became sophisticated through the 1920s, various companies added such refinements as population symbols for towns and cities, indexes, distances between locations, speed limits, and important landmarks and attractions along the way.

By the late 1920s, with the three major companies and several smaller companies working flat out, nearly every oil company was deeply involved with producing and distributing maps to serve the booming tourist trade. There was so much road construction going on at the time, that SOHIO, in 1931, was issuing updated maps three times a year, in April, July, and October. And some of the major oil companies combined with the map companies to set up special travel bureaus at this same time. Before World War II, some 150 million road maps were distributed annually at gas stations.

Beautiful women drivers behind the wheel were an ever-popular and recurrent theme in road map covers from the 1930s. In the 1936 Standard Oil of California map of Arizona and the Richfield Oil example from 1939, the women are whooshing by in their convertibles with windswept hair, while in the splendid 1933 Shell map of New York, the woman at the wheel looks up at us beneath a colorful display of 1933 license plates.

One aspect of road map design, which became a running joke, was how to unfold and refold them within the cramped quarters of a car. Walter Ristow reports that about one hundred different folds were devised and patented. The four most popular folding schemes, as described by Mr. Ristow, are: the accordion fold, most commonly used; the pleat; the sideout; and the combination and diagonal fold. A motorist would have needed a black belt in origami to cope with all these intricate creases.

ROAD MAPS

What was perhaps the most appealing aspect of road map design was not the precise method of cartography, but rather the breathtaking and spectacular commercial art of the road maps' covers. The more eye-catching and attractive the cover, the more the tourist would want a map, and that desire would translate into more sales at the gas station.

By the 1930s, all of the major elements of the road map format had been introduced and perfected, and from then on it was a matter of refinement in production and printing techniques. The popularity of the road map continued unabated except during World War II. From 1914 to 1964, nearly five billion road maps were given out to the American public, and in the years of the 1960s, 200 million maps were distributed annually. In 1972, motorists gobbled up 250 million maps, the most ever.

But then in 1973, the Arab oil embargo hit, and the road map's bubble burst. The death knell had sounded, and by 1978, free road maps had all but disappeared. The very last gasp may have been the closing of Exxon's free public travel office in Rockefeller Center in New York City in 1987.

Nowadays, road maps can be purchased at bookstores and from vending machines at gas stations and convenience stores. And dues-paying AAA members have access to a splendid array of maps, strip maps, and travel guides.

In what were perhaps the most graphically distinguished road maps ever issued in the United States, the Sinclair Refining Company published one spectacular map after another in the decade of the 1930s. One reason the Sinclair maps were so outstanding is that they unfold horizontally into five panels, so that the standard one-panel measurement of 4 by 9 inches exploded into a panoramic cover image 9 inches high by 20 inches wide. And the subject matter and artistic quality of the cover art matched the grandeur of the images' sheer size. Several of the maps in the series, including the Kentucky-Tennessee and Pennsylvania examples, presented precise and highly detailed depictions of Sinclair stations in action. Others, like the New England map cover, used fanciful and hilarious tinted line drawings of stations, dinosaurs, planes, trains, and even a passing float containing the Sinclair Minstrels within a storybook landscape. But the most sensational of all features a panorama of Sinclair Dinosaurs (motor oil "mellowed 100 million years" stated one advertising slogan) against a bright yellow sky, and an explanation inside the map educationally informs us that this is all make-believe because the dinosaurs shown lived during different eras of prehistoric times.

CHAPTER 3

GOLDEN AGE: 1920–1940

By the onset of the 1920s, the automotive boom was going full blast, created by a fortuitous confluence of circumstances and events. More and better roads, a glut of gasoline on the market (the price fell from about 25 cents a gallon to 18 cents during this decade), and a nearly threefold increase in the number of cars (from about eight million in 1920 to some twenty-three million in 1929) were just some of the factors contributing to American automania.

To fuel this increased mobility, there was an explosion in the number of gas stations built in what were, quite literally, the roaring twenties. In 1921 there were some 12,000 drive-in stations operating; this number leaped to 116,000 by 1927, and 143,000 by 1929. Another staggering statistic about gas station growth is that while in 1919 some 47 percent of the gasoline was sold by grocery stores, general stores, and hardware stores, these outlets had virtually disappeared by the end of the 1920s. In 1929 gas and filling stations were selling 91.7 percent of the gasoline produced.

A sailor-suited woman attendant was ready, willing, and able to service gas station customers in Los Angeles in 1926.

A splendid gift thermometer from Lincoln Petroleum in Flint, Michigan, 1925, featured a hand-tinted photograph of a service station and a delivery truck within a custom-sawed wooden frame.

LINCOLN PETROLEUM PRODUCTS COMPANY
FLINT, MICHIGAN
When better Petroleum Products are made
"Lincoln" will supply them.
LINCOLN
PRODUCTS
Pat. 10-13-25
25-614-C.

The office of this 1927 Denver Powerine gas station in Denver was a small building catty-corner to Route 40. But this was a large operation: there were five service bays in a separate building out back.

Letterhead illustration for the Go-Gas Company, New York, New York, 1926.

An illustration from a 1924 *Standard Oil Bulletin* shows one of its red, white, and blue pumps located within an artfully rendered service station interior.

The 1920's Honolulu gas station owned by Olympic swimming medalist Duke Kahanamoku consisted of a fine little office with a pump shelter out front.

"Service stations have sprung up like mushrooms in the last few years and many different types have been introduced," states an article from 1922 in Standard Oil Company of Ohio's magazine, which continues, "some in their newness quite attractive, while others apparently expensive, neither practical or pleasing." An issue of Union Oil's magazine from 1923 is more upbeat, at least about its own stations: "The service station of today is, in many cases, a study in architectural beauty . . . we have stations ranging from the small wooden building with pump in front to what is known as the super service station."

This tiny Union 76 Station in Santa Ana, California, was only a little larger than the three "eye-level" pumps out front.

This "super station" as seen in this 1920s postcard was a very large but architecturally ungainly building.

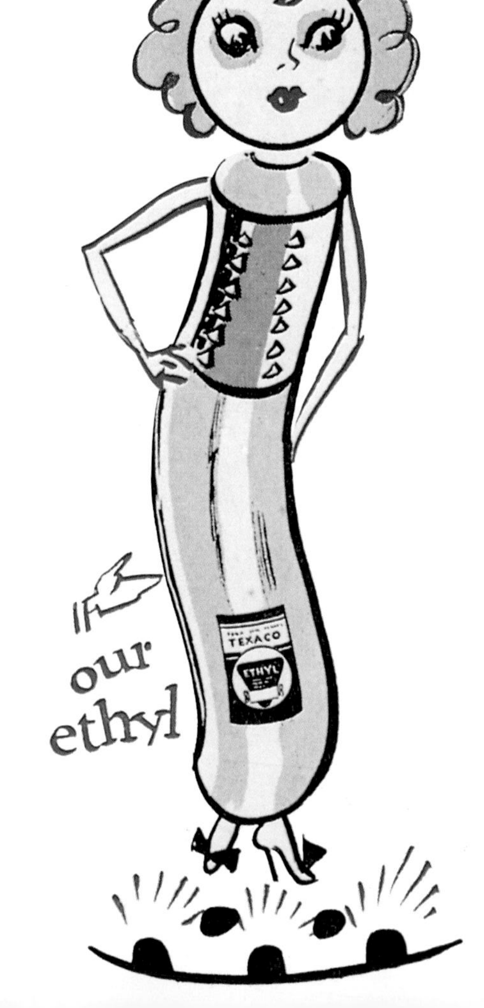

The addition of tetraethyl lead as an antiknocking additive to gasoline beginning in 1923 gave rise to a countless number of "Ethyl" jokes. The "Our Ethyl" illustration from a 1931 Texaco advertising manual is cute and inoffensive, but the sexist joke in the Dude Larsen comic postcard was the most often used variation on the theme.

In the early 1920s many of the gas outlets were unattractive and not very well equipped, but as the decade progressed stations became more sumptuous and extravagant. They evolved boldly from "filling" to "service" stations, this change being one manifestation of the intense competition among too many retail facilities vying for the same dollars. In 1923, tetraethyl lead was introduced as an antiknocking compound in gasoline, and this caused a proliferation of gas pumps — now, in addition to "regular" there was "premium" or "ethyl." Open or semienclosed grease pits were replaced by hydraulic lifts beginning in 1925. The new

This watercolor rendering by architect J. N. Watson for a proposed filling station in suburban Saint Louis in 1921 surpasses the grandeur of the building itself, which is a humble structure with porte cocheres reaching out in three directions.

equipment was often housed in enclosed service bays attached to stations and sometimes euphemistically dubbed "lubritoriums."

The newer, improved stations of this period, in addition to being larger and more attractive, were also characterized by their larger, landscaped lots, wider driveways, and islands with several pumps, sometimes covered by canopies or freestanding shelters. The buildings themselves were often heated and contained "immaculate" restrooms. By the mid-1920s, the sales of automotive equipment (called TBAs in the trade — an acronym for tires, batteries, and accessories) were being promoted, and sales rooms were added to stations. Later in this decade, equipment to wash cars became part of the package.

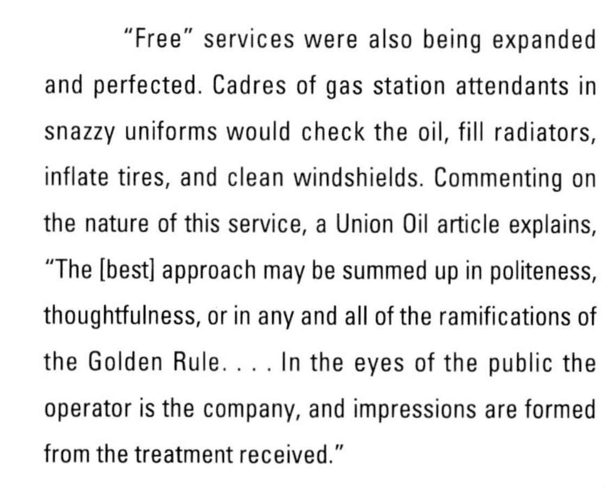

"Free" services were also being expanded and perfected. Cadres of gas station attendants in snazzy uniforms would check the oil, fill radiators, inflate tires, and clean windshields. Commenting on the nature of this service, a Union Oil article explains, "The [best] approach may be summed up in politeness, thoughtfulness, or in any and all of the ramifications of the Golden Rule. . . . In the eyes of the public the operator is the company, and impressions are formed from the treatment received."

Just how hyperextended this notion of "service" had become by the early 1930s can be found in gas station operator Fred Taylor's reply to a survey conducted by Phillips 66. He describes the "Taylor-SERVICE" at his station in Ottawa, Kansas, to which he attributes his increasing sales: "Our explanation for this increase . . . is the unusual 'drive-in' service that other stations in this city do not give. It is a three-man service. Here is how it works: A car drives in on the drive way — we don't wait for him to stop to ask

Gulf gas station attendants lavish attention upon a customer in 1933.

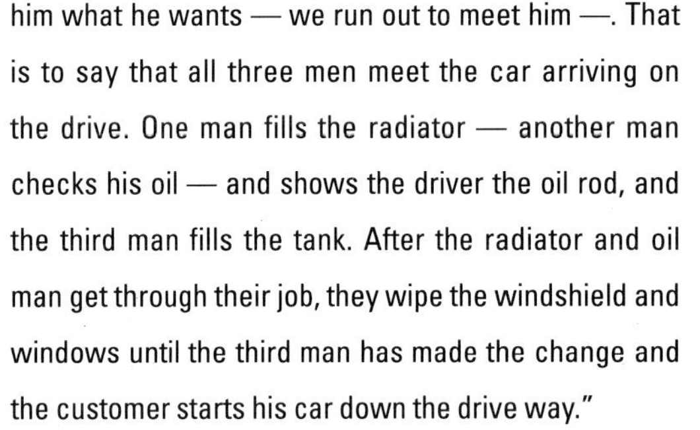

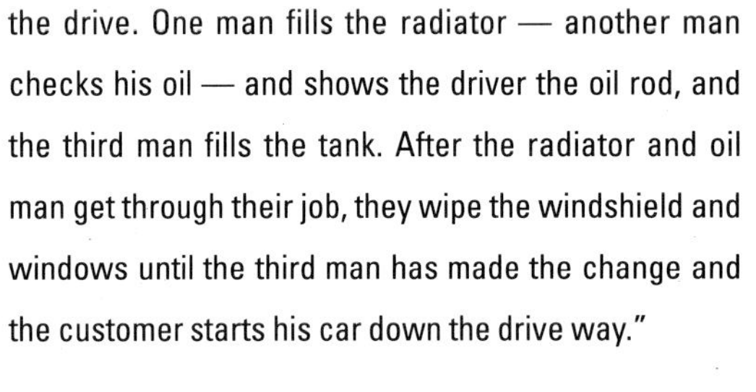

him what he wants — we run out to meet him —. That is to say that all three men meet the car arriving on the drive. One man fills the radiator — another man checks his oil — and shows the driver the oil rod, and the third man fills the tank. After the radiator and oil man get through their job, they wipe the windshield and windows until the third man has made the change and the customer starts his car down the drive way."

The California Petroleum (CALPET) Texaco station on Wilshire Boulevard in Los Angeles was one of the greatest and grandest stations anywhere in the United States. It was designed in 1928 by architect Roland E. Coate, using stuccoed concrete with red, yellow, and black tile trim at its base and on its four-sided dome. A second huge service building was located at the back of the plot. Women service attendants in exotic garb were waiting to serve customers.

The Barnsdall-Rio gas station from 1929 still clings to life in Goleta, California, and keeps alive some of the spirit of the long-gone Calpet palace. The old station in Goleta was designed by Los Angeles architects Morgan, Walls and Clements in high Spanish colonial style.

All of the service and hoopla culminated in the one-stop superstation of the late 1920s. One huge station in Washington, D.C., was operating with fifty-two pumps. And SOHIO came out with its "English Tudor Hunting Lodge" in Cleveland in 1929 — the first of thirty "state of the art" stations to be built. It was an L-shaped building with six service bays, two sales areas, and a women's restroom that rivaled the "lounges" in a movie palace. These one-stop "service

centers," open twenty-four hours a day seven days a week, were the ultimate expression of the gas station craze. Not that many were constructed before the grim reality of the Great Depression set in and required at least a little moderation in approach.

Nonetheless, the trend of "super service stations" continued well into the 1930s. More service bays were added to existing stations, portending a growing emphasis on the auto repair business. There was also more attention given to the marketing of automobile-related products — additional display and sales spaces were incorporated in station design, and display areas were made a part of the pump islands.

In the fury of the gas station building boom, several architectural types emerged that characterized nearly the entire vocabulary of the genre until its demise. Among these types, several had already begun to appear in the first wave of gas station designs.

*The Village Gas-Smith
Beside a tank of gasoline
There stands a hired hand—
He's smeared with oil from honest toil,
He sells 'most ev'ry brand.
And what was once a chestnut tree
Is now a hotdog stand.
—M. C. T., Union, N. J.

A John Held, Jr., map of the United States from a 1929 issue of *The New Yorker* and a prize-winning poem from a 1931 issue of *Super Service Station* magazine provide a clear and humorous picture of the growing number of gas stations and the nature of the roadside environment in general in the boom years of the 1920s and '30s.

This Mobil station added an air of classical elegance to rural Wilson, Kansas. The stucco station had brick quoins and a swan neck pediment above the entrance.

The amorphous and architecturally undistinguished little shacks and sheds were a mainstay of the old days. Because of their ad hoc simplicity and inexpensiveness, little buildings such as these have continued to be utilized through the years. Gas stations were, after all, one of the primary small, individually operated businesses. The little guy with only a couple of pumps out front often wanted just a makeshift shelter-station. These dinky creations cropped up nearly everywhere, and some of the more solidly built examples cling to life today across America.

Prefabricated steel buildings, known as "crackerboxes," were first used in the midteens and proliferated by the thousands in the 1920s. They were eminently practical, inexpensive, and very easy to erect, and one source has described them as the "Model T" of gas stations because of their economy, reliability, and durability. Many oil companies used crackerboxes, although the Shell Oil Company's use of them in California may have been their definitive expression. One account from the early 1920s describes how Shell built some one hundred service stations in six weeks along the 260 miles of road between San Jose and Santa Barbara. Each station took only ten days to construct.

This photograph was taken on the very last day that this brick, English provincial–style building operated as a gas station in Hamilton, New York, in June 1979. Early the next morning, the gas pumps were removed.

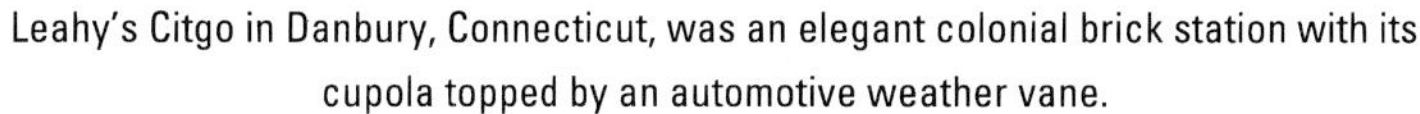

Leahy's Citgo in Danbury, Connecticut, was an elegant colonial brick station with its cupola topped by an automotive weather vane.

Another popular solution for a service station design was to make it look like a little house, proving, once and for all, that a house is not necessarily a home. The house form also helped the station to blend into residential neighborhoods. Two major oil companies, Pure and Phillips, introduced quaint English country cottage–style stations in 1927. Pure Oil introduced its blue-and-white "rain spitter" (so nicknamed because of its steeply pitched blue tile roof) in Indianapolis, complete with window shutters, flower boxes, and a large bay window. The first Phillips cottage opened in Wichita, and by 1930 there were 6,750 of them in twelve states. The Phillips station had a central "chimney" (the Pure model had end chimneys), and each station was painted a distinctive dark green with orange and blue trim to make it stand out from the competition.

A vivid illustration from a Shell road map depicts a typical "crackerbox" gas station.

The Phillips Petroleum Company opened its first English cottage station in Wichita, Kansas, in 1927, and spread the design across the Midwest. It was shaped like a house to fit into residential neighborhoods, but it had an assertive orange and green shingled roof to attract attention, as seen in details from two Phillips road map covers. A survivor into the 1970s in Turkey, Texas, with its distinctive central chimney, had its colorful roof replaced.

The Pure Oil Company was the other major oil company to have a standardized, house-form design for their stations. Their design, as seen in a detail from a road map cover, has flanking chimneys, shutters, and flower boxes.

While the Pure and Phillips stations utilized traditional architectural styles to establish their identities, just as SOHIO had done with its superstations, many other major oil companies called upon a full range of decorative eclecticism to establish regional and national identities for their building programs. Until World War II, the Gulf Oil Company built in styles suitable to the area where the station was located — colonial in the Northeast and Spanish stucco in Florida and California. The Jenney Oil Company in New England and Standard Oil of New York produced various types of "colonial" visions, while the Ventura Oil Company in Los Angeles opted for a mission-style design.

The final, and by far the most entertaining and intriguing, design type for the gas station was the building in the shape of a recognizable object. Sometimes the shape of the building made sense because of its petroleum imagery. There were gas pump–shaped stations in Maryville, Missouri, and Lancaster, Pennsylvania, and an oil can–shaped station in Buchanan, New York. In the 1920s there was a chain of shell-shaped Shell stations in North Carolina, one of which survived and was placed on the National Register of Historic Places.

The McClesky Bros. service station, Birmingham, Alabama, 1932, probably never looked as good as it does here in this artful and superbly hand-tinted photograph.

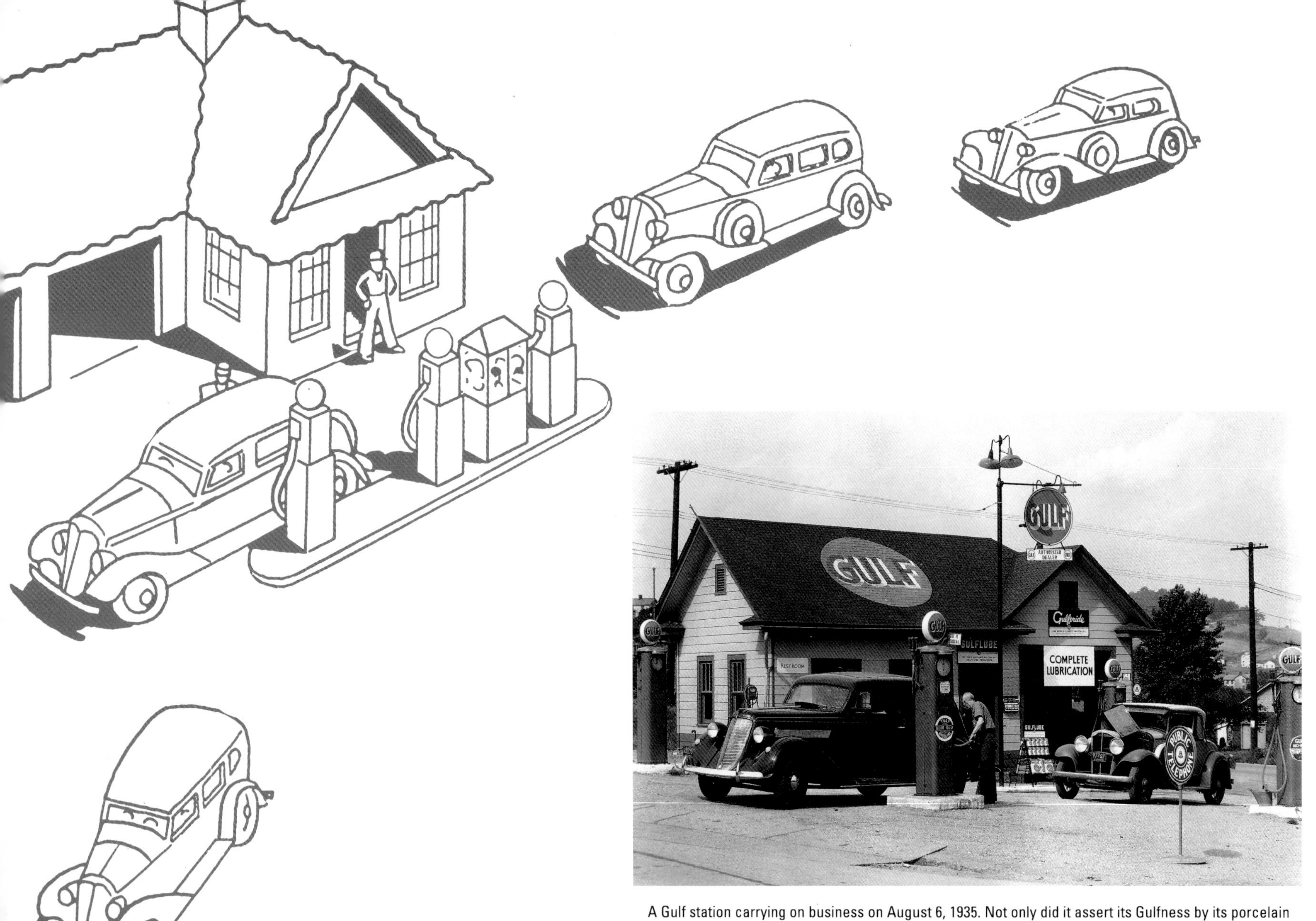

A Gulf station carrying on business on August 6, 1935. Not only did it assert its Gulfness by its porcelain enamel sign hung perpendicular to the road, but by a disc painted on the roof.

Others of these stations made less sense symbolically, although for commercially practical purposes they were definitely hard to miss. There have been iceberg-shaped stations in Ottawa, Kansas, Roanoke, Alabama, and Albuquerque, New Mexico; many a windmill and tepee; and lighthouses galore as recognizable beacons amidst the seas of roadside traffic.

Gas stations, great and small, grand and mundane, continued to multiply as the era of the Great Depression loomed. But, concentrating upon the gas station phenomenon alone, one might have logically posed the question "What depression?" The overbuilding of gas stations in the 1920s was exceeded only by the building boom of the 1930s. There were 143,000 retail outlets for gas in 1929, 170,000 by 1933, and this number ballooned to a staggering 231,000 in 1940.

Because there were so many gas stations — it seemed that one cropped up nearly every block or two in an urban area — the competition for customers accelerated. Uniforms and services became more elaborate, advertising campaigns in magazines, news-

The Devil's Elbow Cafe and Conoco Station, in all of its stony splendor, seen here in a 1930s real-photo postcard, beckoned to passersby along Route 66 in rural Missouri.

papers, and on radio became more intense and omnipresent, and promotional giveaways more numerous and lavish.

The new and almost necessary trend in gas station design was not to blend in, but to stick out and demand customer attention. This increased emphasis upon architectural self-expression is echoed in a statement in a 1941 issue of Gulf's *Orange Disc* magazine: "Today the motorist can pass by the unattractive, out-of-date gasoline station and drive on for many miles to an up-to-date, attractive station for the products he needs. One glance at the station will tell him what he may expect. He has learned that the modern station is where he can find the most complete selection of products, the best lubrication and car washing facilities, a complete stock of tires and accessories, and above all the courteous, well-trained attendants who can service his car in the proper manner."

Tank car–shaped stations were symbolic of cut-rate gasoline in the 1930s. Bill's Service Station in Creston, Iowa, was a building shaped like a tank car, while the Premier Tank Car Stations matchbook cover, below, had tanks on either end and the low-price slogan, "tank car to you," on the station's facade.

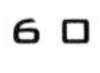

The other major marketing trend that emerged in the 1930s was the so-called trackside operation where gas was dispensed at cut-rate prices on a no-frills basis. Usually the gas was sold from an actual railroad tank car sitting on the tracks, although sometimes the tank cars were moved to tracks beside the road or a building was constructed in the shape of a tank car. But the whole idea of cut-rate, no-frills marketing, which was accompanied by the emergence of private brand companies, which became known as "independents," foreshadowed the coming era of self-service and the eventual decline of the service station itself.

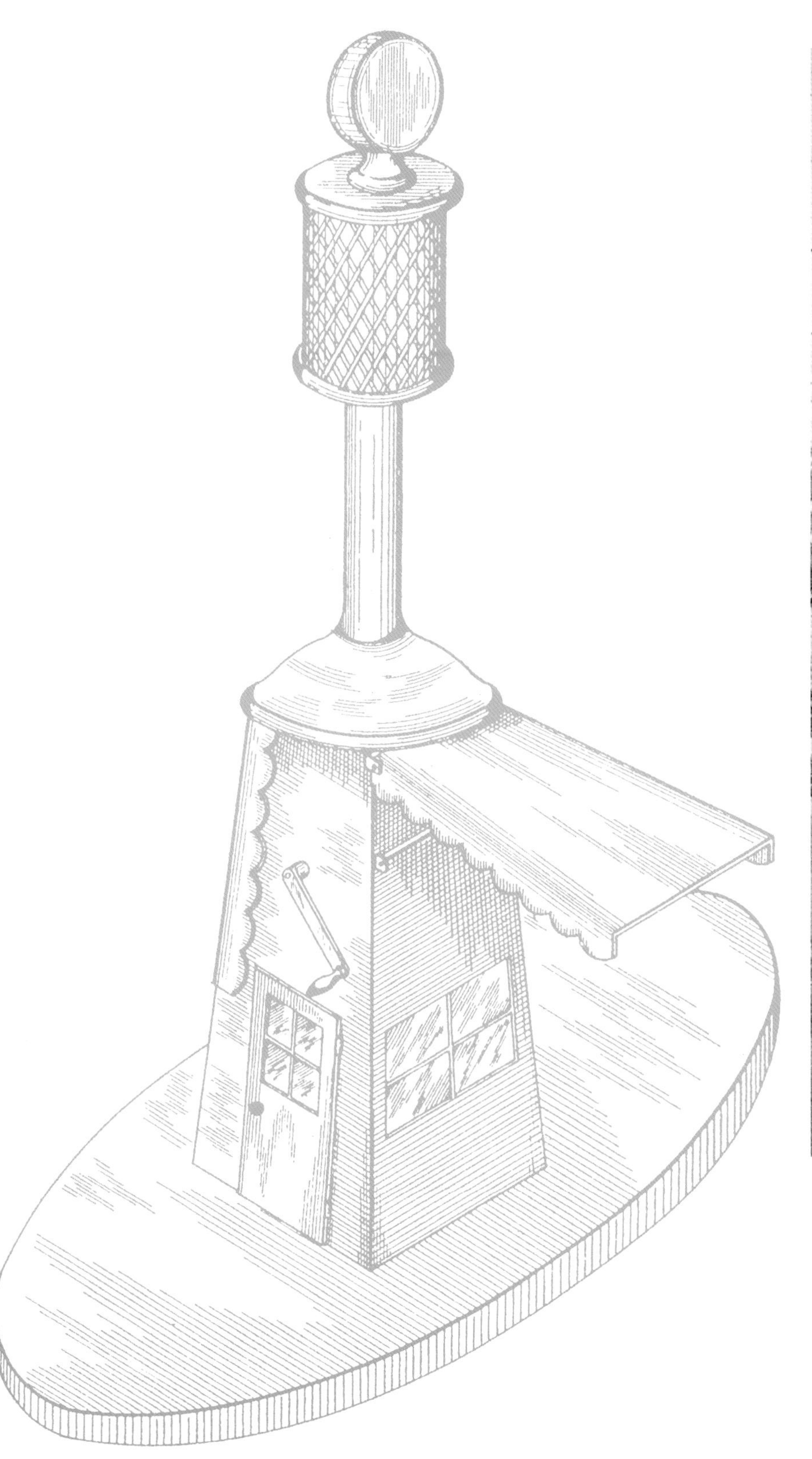

A gas station shaped like a gas pump was another inescapably direct expression of what the business was all about. One Ross McCoy of Alameda, California, was granted a patent for this idea in 1929. And a "Big Pump" station in Maryville, Missouri, seen here in a postcard view, was still in operation in the 1970s.

The Beautiful GULF LIGHTHOUSE SERVICE STATION County Causeway . . . Miami Beach, Florida

The tank car station, real or fabricated, did continue the entertaining trend of bizarre and idiosyncratic service station designs. In what was perhaps the most outstanding example of "Pop" architecture in this era was a lighthouse station built by Gulf at the terminus of the Dade County Causeway in Miami Beach in 1938. An article in Gulf's *Orange Disc* magazine of that year tells us that it was a "beautiful and imposing" building "acclaimed by many as 'the swankiest service station in the world.'"

The advent of World War II marked the end of a grand and glorious era in the history of the gas station. Indeed, it marked the end of an age of idealism and innocence in American culture. Never again would there be the fervor and zeal of the free-enterprise system so sumptuously and joyously expressed in commercial design. The new reality after the war would be more ascetic, economical, and practical, and what little joy remained in the commercial environment would be expressed in scaled-back imitations of the big-time hoopla of the "wonder years" from 1920 to 1940.

The idea of a lighthouse-shaped gas station is a mixed metaphor. Instead of warning ships of dangers, these roadside beacons, siren-like, called out to motorists by their shape rather than their meaning. The most famous lighthouse station must have been the Gulf station by the County Causeway in Miami along the Intracoastal Waterway, seen here in a linen postcard view. Gulf-described as "the swankiest station in the world," this tour de force also contained a bar, restaurant, and hotel rooms. A patent was granted to a man in Ohio in 1926 for this same idea, above, and the Colonial Beacon Gas Company, left, had a series of lighthouse stations dating from the 1930s located throughout New York State, including one in Eaton, New York, which went on to become a restaurant.

The Nehi bottle gas station, 64 feet high and 49 feet in diameter, existed only from 1924 to 1935 just north of Opelika, Alabama. Before it burned to the ground, the huge wooden bottle had a gas station and grocery store on ground level, a two-level living quarters, and a spiral stairway to the 16-foot-diameter cap, which served as an observation deck.

The Teapot Dome Service Station in Zillah, Washington, was built in 1922 as a reminder of the famous political scandal. The circular frame building with a conical roof, sheet metal handle, and concrete spout, was moved 1.2 miles to its present site in 1978 and placed on the National Register of Historic Places. It still operates as a beloved gas station, and it also has bird houses for sale.

Windmill-shaped buildings were another popular solution for designing an eye-catching gas station. In the 1920s in Saint Cloud, Minnesota, the Home Oil Company operated a cute little Deep Rock Gasoline station, while a windmill in Ellensburg, Washington, above, still operating in the 1970s, was abandoned by 1991 but still there.

POP ARCHITECTURE

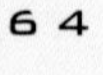

Gas stations were among the most often found buildings along the roadside commercial environment of America. Some enterprising roadside entrepreneurs chose to build oversized replicas of recognizable objects to make their gas stations stand out from all the rest. What to call these spectacular roadside metaphors is another matter. Architects Robert Venturi and Denise Scott Brown have dubbed them "ducks" (after a duck-shaped building in Riverhead, New York, which was selling, what else, ducks). Architectural historian David Gebhard refers to them as "programmatic" buildings, and others called them mimetic architecture. And Andy Warhol might have called them Pop Architecture. But, whatever they are called, they are certainly a fantastic and pervasive tradition in American commercial design, and a tradition in gas stations that has prevailed, with less and less frequency, even into the 1960s and 1970s.

HOME OIL
GASOLINE
DEEP ROCK
COMPANY
1924

An "iceberg"-shaped gas station on the northern edge of Ottawa, Kansas, was one of several of its genre built and operated throughout the United States. Built in the 1930s, it was still selling gas in the mid-1970s.

About eight shell-shaped concrete Shell gas stations were built in the Winston-Salem, North Carolina, area in the early 1930s. This one survivor, 18 feet high, no longer sells gas, but it was placed on the National Register of Historic Places.

The Hat and Boots Gas Station on Highway 99 in Seattle was built just after World War II. The hat, with its sheltering 45-foot-wide brim, housed the offices, and the boots were homes for the restrooms.

This 110-foot-long dinosaur was built as a Sinclair Gas station in the mid-1960s. Constructed of sprayed concrete and 34 feet high at the head, the huge building has three arched service bays.

A 50-foot-high tepee gas station built in 1930 was the centerpiece of an Indian Village complex on Highway 40 in Lawrence, Kansas. It was still operating as an Amoco station in the mid-1970s, but closed shortly thereafter.

There were other tepee gas stations operating throughout the United States, including one from about 1930 seen in a real-photo postcard from Corwin Hot Springs, Montana, complete with a tepee-ette pump shelter.

As a tribute to our brave pilots in World War II, Art Lacey created his Bomber Gas Station in Milwaukie, Oregon, by raising an old B-17 above rows of gas pumps along old Highway 99.

AIRCRAFT

Perhaps the strangest symbolic design link is the marriage of the airplane to the gasoline station. Although the semiotic meaning between the two is blurred at best, the airplane's shape is particularly well suited for the design of a service station because the wings serve as protective canopies for sheltering the gas pumps, while the cockpit becomes the office. The flying saucer profile shares similar functional advantages. And whatever the type of aircraft employed, all have the distinct advantage of being unforgettable icons in the busy clutter of the roadside environment.

Bob's Airmail Service, a 32-passenger Fokker plane with a 100-foot wing span, held forth along Wilshire Boulevard in Los Angeles in the 1930s. It had neon-lighted wings and revolving propellers, and customers could tour the plane's interior.

Owner and designer Ray Keyes conceived of this flying saucer gas station on Highway 20 in Ashtabula, Ohio, in 1966. The roof was used for storage and heating, while the stem housed the office, rest rooms, and a service center. An alien (left), who might just have arrived in Ohio in the 1960s, staked out a space in front of a gas station–car wash in Los Angeles in 1975.

A zeppelin-shaped building grounded beside the Lincoln Highway near Pittsburgh served triple duty as a Pennzoil gas station, restaurant, and tourist camp office.

An old biplane-shaped gas station now serves other functions on the outskirts of Knoxville, Tennessee.

L. E. Agan opened his first gas station on Highway 67 West in Texarkana, Texas, after World War II. When he rebuilt this Stop-Agan station he exercised his knowledge of roadside marketing by plunking a large plane on top of his building, as seen in this 1952 photograph. And he placed a huge rabbit statue covered with lamb's wool out front so tourists could pose with it for a memorable photo opportunity. The station closed in the late 1950s, but the rabbit is still there in front of yet another new building, Big Daddy's Pawn Shop, run by Agan's daughter.

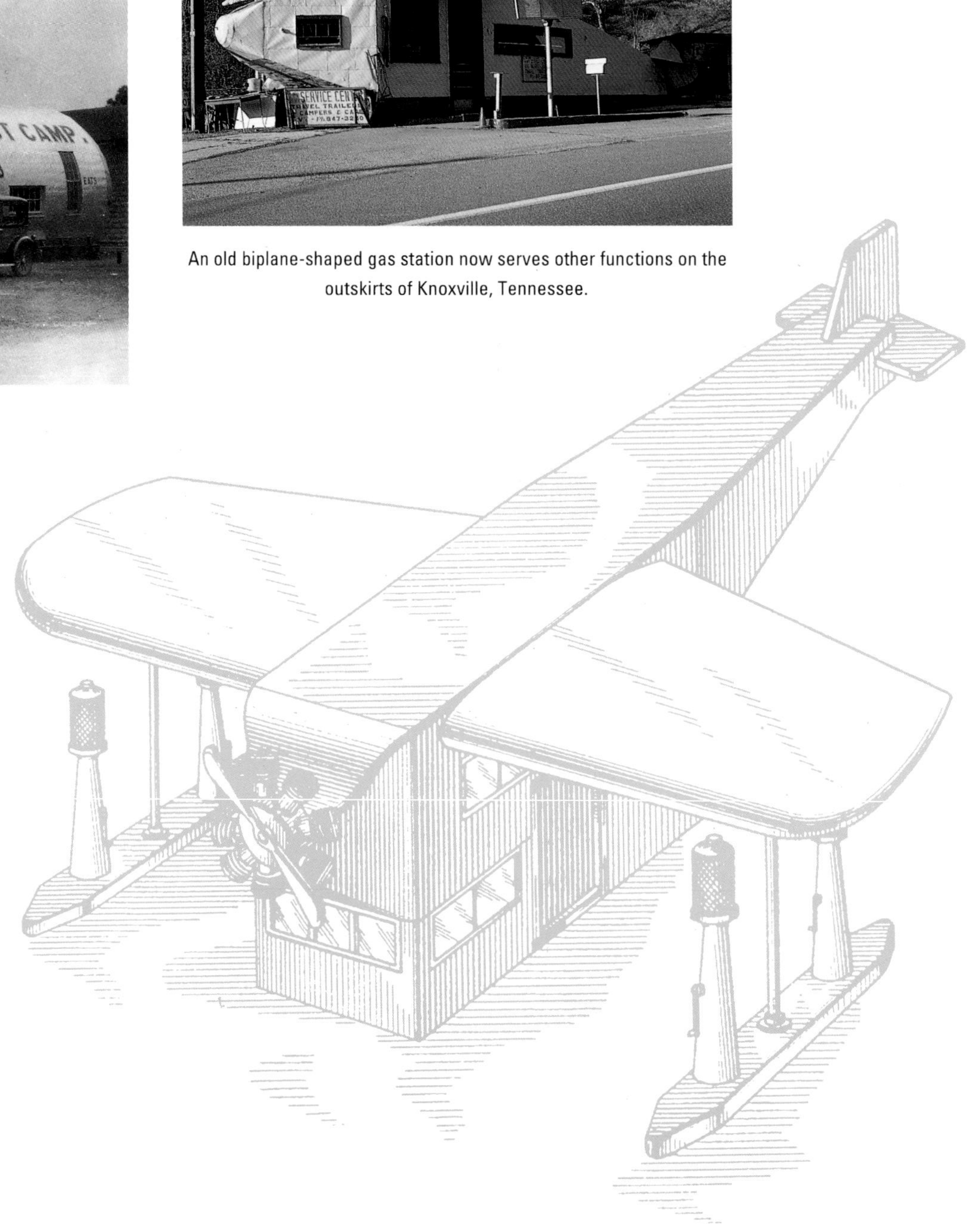

C. D. Vary of Elgin, Illinois, was granted a patent in 1930 for this "ornamental design for a portable gasoline filling station booth."

The Zenith Albatross Texaco Station was a gas outlet located near Hollywood, California. This airplane, built by Kingsford Smith, broke a nonstop flight record in 1926.

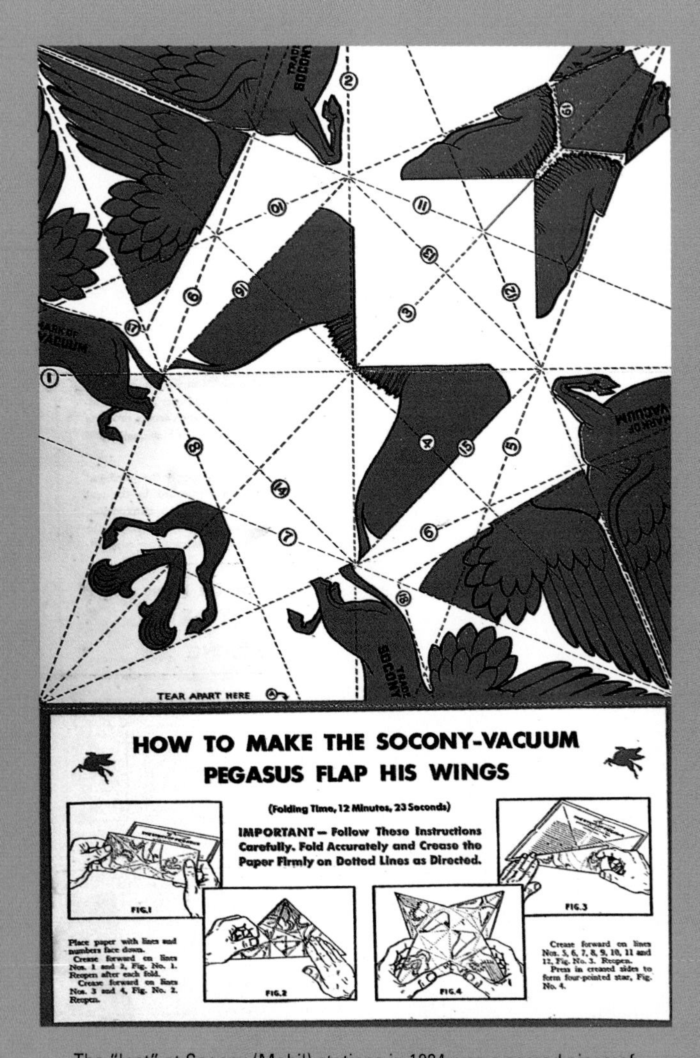

The "loot" at Socony (Mobil) stations in 1934 was a scored piece of cardboard that could be folded into a small, wing-flapping replica of the famous Pegasus symbol.

Many oil companies gave away different versions of auto bingo games to entertain kids as they were being driven around. "Sight-O" was Mobil's 1959 variation on this theme.

"The Man Who Salutes," a friendly white-uniformed gas station attendant, became a graphic symbol for Standard Oil of California in 1931. When the company opened a new station, children were given this mechanical cardboard replica of "the man." When the tab at the bottom was pulled, he saluted.

KID STUFF
RAZZMATAZZ

As gas stations fought to establish commercial viability in a raging sea of intense competition, someone came up with the great idea of giving neat stuff to kids so their parents world return time after time to buy more and more gas. The kids of the 1920s and the '30s were the lucky ones. They got neat board games and cutout models, among other treasures. After World War II, the pickings were slimmer but still amiable.

Some fortunate kids who visited Shell stations in 1936 were given the cardboard "Stop and Go" game complete with cutout game pieces, Super Shell gas tickets, and a wheel with an attached metal spinner. The object of the game was to get "home" first.

The World's Largest Redwood Tree Service Station was built in the mid-1930s along Highway 101, the Redwood Highway, a place of tall trees and tourist attractions. It remains pretty much intact even to this day, but now it is a beloved landmark. Gas is pumped from a newer station immediately adjacent to the big stump relic.

BELIEVE IT OR NOT!

Pride, wonder, and entrepreneurial enthusiasm all came together in this self-proclaimed superlative group of gas stations. These outlets with the mostest certainly didn't wish to keep their unique distinctions a secret. And so, sometimes by signs and more often by the issuing of colorful postcards to be distributed by customers, proud gas stations owners "told the world" about their own, very special eighth wonders.

THE MOST ARTISTIC IN THE U.S.A.: This log cabin and half-timbered station in Fergus Falls, Minnesota, attributes its distinction to "national tourist proclamation." One tourist's message of the back of this postcard admires the red, white, and blue electric lights strung around the edges of the building.

THE MOST BEAUTIFUL IN THE SOUTH: This Cities Service Station in Shreveport, Louisiana, boasts that it is "illuminated at night by more than a mile of the neon tubing" and that is a "radiant and colorful spectacle."

THE MOST BEAUTIFUL SERVICE STATION IN THE SOUTH

KOOLMOTOR OILS · GASOLENE

ACME

WASHING - POLISHING

9A-H2329

FAIRFIELD AND JORDAN STREETS — SHREVEPORT, LOUISIANA

THE LARGEST CO-OP STATION IN IOWA: No information is provided to back up the claim of the Plymouth Co-Op Oil Company station in LeMars, Iowa, seen here in a stunning linen postcard from the 1940s. But off to the left can be seen at least six and maybe seven service bays. So this was a very large operation.

THE MOST BEAUTIFUL IN AMERICA: The Central Texaco station doesn't give any backup information to support its claim to fame, but it is a very fine-looking and imposing structure.

Cities Service was but one of the oil companies with their own orchestras performing regular radio programs. Paul Lavalle, before he went on to head the McDonald's All-American Band, is seen here in 1950 leading the Cities Service Band of America before a Belasco Theater, New York City, live audience of 950 people and a coast-to-coast radio audience.

THAT'S ENTERTAINMENT!

RAZZMATAZZ

In the early 1950s the Union Oil Company was seeking a new way to promote the sales of its Royal Trition Motor Oil, a purple-hued goo. Their solution was to hire Marilyn Monroe, who, in her only television commercial ever, gushed to an eager attendant to add a quart of oil to the "tummy" of her pink convertible. In the 1930s Mickey Mouse and Donald Duck expressed their preference for Sunoco products.

Other oil companies have sponsored cultural programs or associated themselves with celebrities as a means of building goodwill and increasing sales. Beginning in the 1920s, the Pure Oil Company and Cities Service had their own bands with programs on the NBC radio network. And Texaco has continuously sponsored Metropolitan Opera radio broadcasts since 1940.

And it is also Texaco that has been the leader of the band of oil companies in the show-biz biz. The company has enlisted the services of a "Who's Who" of celebrity spokespersons, beginning with Ed Wynn in 1933 and continuing with the likes of Fred Allen, Eddie Cantor, Jack Benny, Jimmy Durante , and, more recently, Bob Hope. And the first generation of television viewers will never forget the singing Merry Texaco Men as they introduced Uncle Miltie every Tuesday night across America.

Comedian Ed Wynn, "the perfect fool," became the first Texaco Fire Chief on the company's first radio program on April 26, 1933, by uttering the line: "Ladies and Gentlemen, on behalf of the Texaco Company — and I'd like to be half of the Texaco Company. . . ." His reign as Fire Chief lasted through 1935, and he was charmingly portrayed by illustrator Will Cotton in a 1934 magazine ad, and further promoted by giveaways like an Ed Wynn mask.

The famous singing Texaco Quartet opened the Texaco Star Theater TV Show in the late 1940s by introducing Milton Berle with a rousing rendition of their famous song:

Oh, we're the men of Texaco.
We work from Maine to Mexico.
There's nothing like this Texaco of ours.
Our show tonight is powerful.
We'll wow you with an hour-full
Of howls from a showerful of stars.
We're the Merry Texaco Men.
Tonight we may be show men,
Tomorrow we'll be servicing your cars.

FIRST MAN: I wipe the pipe, I pump the gas,
I rub the hub, I scrub the glass.

SECOND MAN I touch the clutch, I poke the choke.

THIRD MAN: I clear the gear, I block the knock,
I jack the back, I set the clock.

FOURTH MAN: So join the ranks of those who know,
And fill your tanks with Texaco.

ALL: Sky Chief — fill up with Sky Chief,
And you will smile at the pile of
new miles you will add.
Fire Chief — fill up with Fire Chief.
You'll find that Texaco's the finest
friend your car has ever had!

Fifteen major oil companies joined forces to build this impressive edifice at the 1939 New York World's Fair. The building, seen here as reproduced from a special Shell World's Fair road map, graphically represented the history of the American oil industry.

THAT'S ENTERTAINMENT!
RAZZMATAZZ

Advertising and promotional materials were produced by oil companies with one major objective in mind — to increase sales and profits. But the road to increased profits was also paved with good intentions. Imaginative commercial artifacts were given away "for free."

Various world's fairs and expositions and major athletic events presented a perfect opportunity for public-relations-conscious oil and gas companies. There was so much goodwill to be shared...and promoted.

The Magnolia Petroleum Company, which became part of Mobil Oil, built a lounge "for the comfort and pleasure of visitors" to the 1936 Texas Centennial Exposition in Dallas, and then at the Pan American Exposition.

Elephants performed at the Standard Oil exhibit at the 1933–1934 Century of Progress Exposition in Chicago. The "I Got Live Power" slogan was a link to Standard's advertising campaign of that time.

A booklet for the Sinclair Dinoland exhibit at the New York World's Fair of 1964–1965 gave visitors insights into the history of these fabled, extinct creatures.

The Richfield Oil Company did its part during the 1932 Olympic Games held in Los Angeles. It dispatched a Scout Car with a public address system manned by two nattily attired traffic control operators.

The Tower Service Station, built in 1936, reaches to the sky to attract motorists at its intersection location on Route 66 in Shamrock, Texas. It is seen here with its garish red, white, and blue Bicentennial paint job.

A tapered, cylindrical tower creates a distinctive identity for this old Union 76 station in Tucson, Arizona.

DECO–MODERNE

The latest and the greatest stylistic innovations of the 1930s were Art Deco and Streamline Moderne. These styles were intentional abstractions meant to connote modernity. Buildings had a new fluidity, with windswept curvilinear corners. In the horizontal mode, a streamlined building approximated the image and romance of a speeding locomotive passing by beside the road. In vertical configuration, towers swept skyward like the vapor streams of a Flash Gordon rocket ship. But whether vertical or horizontal, many of these snazzy gems could well have served as stage sets for a production number from a Busby Berkeley musical. And with only a little fanciful imagination, one can clearly picture Fred Astaire and Ginger Rogers swirling out of a service bay in the frenzy of one of their dancing displays.

The Direct Service gas station in Minneapolis, 1937, was built of glass block, an almost ideal material for curvilinear streamlining. By day, sunlight would gleam and reflect from the glass surface, while at night a lighting system transformed the building into a glowing red temple of petroleum.

When Lee and Julian Field returned from World War I, they built one of the first gas stations between Oklahoma City and Dallas in 1919 in Pauls Valley, Oklahoma, and they remodeled the building into up-to-date Art Moderne splendor in the late 1930s. Lee Jr. took over the business in the 1950s and kept it going until 1983, when, because the building had been bypassed by the interstate highway and because new self-serves reigned supreme, he sold out. The new owner went bankrupt, and now the building stands empty.

A six-towered Art Deco Cities Service station in Arkansas glimmers in the nighttime light, with its symmetrical design spelling out the services it was offering.

A masterfully designed Gulf station in Miami, Florida, is dominated by the profile of its automobile spring columns supporting two porte cocheres. The Deco composition is enhanced by glass block strips and cool vent awnings.

The Somerset Service Station, Mountainside, New Jersey, used glass block accents and painted stripes of color to achieve its spiffy profile.

CHAPTER 4

"GOING, GOING..."

1940-1965

A Sohioette at work in World War II.

With the outbreak of World War II, everything else became insignificant immediately. Construction of service stations came to a halt. Many of the men who worked at gas stations went to war, sometimes to be replaced by a female cadre of gas station attendants.

But the greatest impact of the war was the shortage of rubber and gasoline, as these vital commodities were channeled into the military effort. Gas rationing was instituted nationwide on December 1, 1942 — a convoluted and ultimately effective system using various coupon books, further complicated by cheats and chiselers, gangster activity, and a flourishing black market.

After World War II, America got back behind the wheel and once again began to pile up the miles with a passion: in 1941 gas stations sales were three and one-half billion gallons; in 1951 this consumption

had nearly tripled to over eight billion gallons. An ominous milestone came in 1948, when, for the first time, the United States became a net importer of crude oil, as our thirst for gasoline surpassed our own supply. Twenty-five years later, the significance of this moment would become all too clear.

Why is this woman smiling? On May 15, 1942, when East Coast gas rationing was just one minute old, Elizabeth Berry made the first purchase of rationed gas from Jack Felderman's gas station.

ESSO
DEALER

A gleaming porcelain enamel "drum"-type Mobilgas station in Mount Clemens, Michigan, 1947, was based upon a 1940 design by architect Frederick Frost.

The postwar period was a time of rapid suburban expansion, and with it a new generation of gas stations. At first there was a continuation of the porcelain enamel on metal panel boxlike stations so popular in the late 1930s. In the 1940s the stations evolved into cleaner, more efficient design statements, with aluminum accents and all-glass fronts. Some companies continued their regional design styling.

Other major oil companies hired some of the best American designers to come up with new station designs in the late 1930s and the 1940s. Architect Frederick Frost designed the "drum"-type porcelain enamel station for Mobil in 1940, called that because of its rounded corner office. Walter Dorwin Teague had developed a prototype for Texaco in the 1930s, and Raymond Loewy was conceiving new design ideas for Shell and Union Oil.

Business was proceeding as usual in the 1950s at this Flying A station, probably located in or near Wilmington, Delaware, as a now classic Oldsmobile gets a tankful of 100 octane fuel dispensed from an "eye-level" pump.

The "service" in service stations was still an important factor in the gas stations of the 1950s. Phillips 66 published a small, hardcover book in 1955 titled *Service Station Operation and Selling.* It described the "10 steps to perfect pump island service." Among these ten steps, many of them the predictable filling, checking, and cleaning, one special activity stands out — whisk broom service, a service the manual describes as having a special appeal to women. "Of all the services offered on the driveway none is quite so impressive as the removal of accumulated dirt from the floor of the car," the Phillips attendant was told. "A whisk broom properly used should prove to be the most productive good will building tool around the service station." These were certainly still the good old days.

Klieg lights shone in the sky and strung pennants fluttered in the breeze at the opening of this Standard station in northern California or southern Oregon in the late 1940s.

After World War II, canopies staged a comeback in gas station design as demonstrated by Phil Blanco's Conoco station in Houston, shown here in an original photograph (with its now-stained label) used to produce a postcard.

But slowly and inevitably, assertive designs were replaced by models that blended in with the new suburbs. Ranch-style stations were very popular, with roof overhangs and darker colors. Other rustic materials were utilized, like cedar shakes and "old" used brick.

By the late 1950s and into the 1960s, gas stations became more and more stripped down and functional. Most companies adopted simple, economical standardized design solutions. Cinder block and concrete block replaced prefabricated steel as the least expensive building material of choice. By the 1960s, molded plastic was being used to imitate real building materials.

Sowell-Simon

Wally Mason poses in the salesroom of his service station in Washington Township, New Jersey, in the 1950s. Since the 1930s, tires, batteries, and accessories (TBAs in trade jargon) had become an increasingly important part of the gas station business.

Car-Saver Service illustration from a 1947 *Texaco Dealer* magazine.

Except for opening day, this lubrication bay of a Boston Chevrolet dealership was probably never as immaculate and spotless as it was in this 1941 photograph.

And canopies reappeared with a vengeance. The box designs of the 1930s and 1940s had eliminated canopies. They were a distraction from the flowing lines and contrasting colors of the station designs. The new canopies became longer and longer, and sometimes there were two canopies. Some of them swept upward like tail fins on 1950s automobiles, and there were so-called butterfly canopies used as devices to display huge advertising signs mounted on top of them. By the 1960s, there were even freestanding canopies.

The new stations had lost the verve and élan of earlier decades. They were symptomatic of a new era in American business when less and less was more and more. Efficiency and economy replaced individuality. The new automotive strips became vitiated, tasteful ghosts of their former gaudy splendor. The old, content-laden corporate logos, which had used animals and other imagery much like mascots for college football teams, were put out to pasture and replaced by abstract symbols or huge-scale sans serif lettering. So-called good taste was having a devastating effect upon the roadside environment.

CHROME CLEANER POLISH
RUST PREVENTIVE
RUBBER LUBRICANT
A NEW BATTERY... deserves NEW CABLES
TIDEWATER OIL COMPANY
AIR WING TUBE
FLYING A QUALITY
AIR WING TUBE
FLYING A SERVICE
Tidewater Oil Company
FLYING A TIRES Longer, Safer Mileage
FLYING A TIRES Longer, Safer Mileage

Renowned sports writer Grantland Rice worked with Cities Service Gasoline in 1948 and several years thereafter to compile a football guide given out to customers.

Cities Service was one of many gas companies to give away plastic gas pump–shaped salt and pepper shakers as promotional inducements.

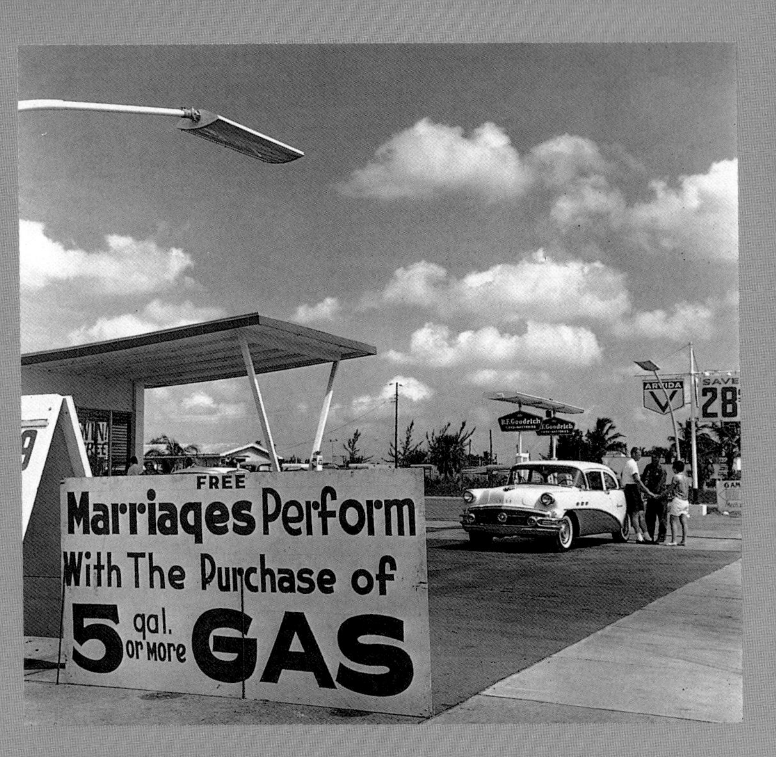

POST-WAR FROLICS

Razzmatazz

Gimmicks, giveaways, and promotional fervor continued with a new enthusiasm as Americans once again took to the road with a passion after World War II. Accompanying the new surge in service station construction was a new wave of "free gifts" and other goodies to woo and win new customers.

In one mind-boggling promotional scheme in Miami, Florida, in 1961, gas station owner Wally Smith became a notary public and offered to perform marriage ceremonies for free with the purchase of five or more gallons of gas. The first happy couple took their vows beside the gas pumps. One couple chose to take their vows while standing on top of the grease rack, which Wally had cleaned off for the occasion, but the lucky groom nearly fell off when he leaned over to kiss the bride. Another couple was married on the roof of the station, while yet another duo chose to say their "I dos" while stand atop the narrow confines of the soda machine.

Pearl Mann and Richard Alkine were the very first couple to get a free marriage ceremony from Wally Smith at his gas station in Miami, in August 1961.

FREE GIFTS
FREE GIFTS

Clowns galore, bedecked in uniforms featuring the company logo, gathered at a "school" in a Nashville, Tennessee, hotel meeting room before presiding at the simultaneous opening of twenty-four Phillips 66 stations in Memphis in 1956.

Lawrence Stiff opened his gas station in Lovelock, Nevada, in 1924 and brought his father, Ed, into the business in 1938. The "Two Stiffs Selling Gas" logo was then invented, seen here on a linen postcard from the 1940s. The two "hobo" types also existed as statues in front of the gas station. Lawrence Stiff died in the 1980s, and now the "Two Stiffs" statues stand in high decay in front of a convenience store.

Neat decks of Tydol playing cards were an incentive for customers to fill up with Flying A in the 1950s.

POST-WAR FROLICS

RAZZMATAZZ

The use of clowns by the Phillips Petroleum Company as an extra added attraction in the hoopla of opening new stations first began in Tampa, Florida, in 1953. And then the sales department decided to make them a part of every station's premiere. Late in 1954, the company decided to have the costumes made of specially designed Phillips 66 fabric of orange, black, and white emblazoned with the company's logo. Clown mania peaked in 1956 when a corps of twenty-four buffoons, usually portrayed by sales trainees, presided at the simultaneous opening of twenty-four stations in Memphis, Tennessee.

Buzz's Skelly Station, Colorado Springs, Colorado, is seen here in 1980 with its tiles gleaming in the early morning light. The building, constructed in 1950, was closed in 1981. Now with the facade painted dull gray, the building is used as a car rental office.

PORCELAIN ENAMEL

Porcelain enamel tile was a building material perfectly suited for use in gas stations. It was inexpensive (at least it was then) and it was durable and nearly maintenance-free. Its baked enamel surface was impervious to damage, and it could be easily cleaned by hosing it off, or washing it like a car itself until the shine returned from beneath the grease and grime.

The N. J. Brown station in Kingsland, Georgia, was a typical Gulf "ice box."

This handsome gas station in Connersville, Indiana, with its flashy upwardly tapering tower, was most certainly "Modern" when it was built decades ago. But by 1980 when this photograph was taken, the station was a Moderne and well-preserved relic of earlier times.

"Oklahoma" was certainly a great name for this tile station in Detroit, because southwestern oil helped Motown wheels to roll. By 1987 the station was out of the gas business, but automobiles were still being repaired on the premises.

The porcelain enamel era lasted from the 1930s into the 1950s, and by the tasteful 1960s, these durable and eye-catching outlets were "remodeled" by removing the tile and transforming the buildings into suburban ranch-style stations to blend in with newer suburbs. Most of the rest were razed and replaced. A few survivors, resplendent colorful compositions, house other businesses. But the porcelain enamel panels, fifty or sixty years old, gleam away as if they had been installed last year.

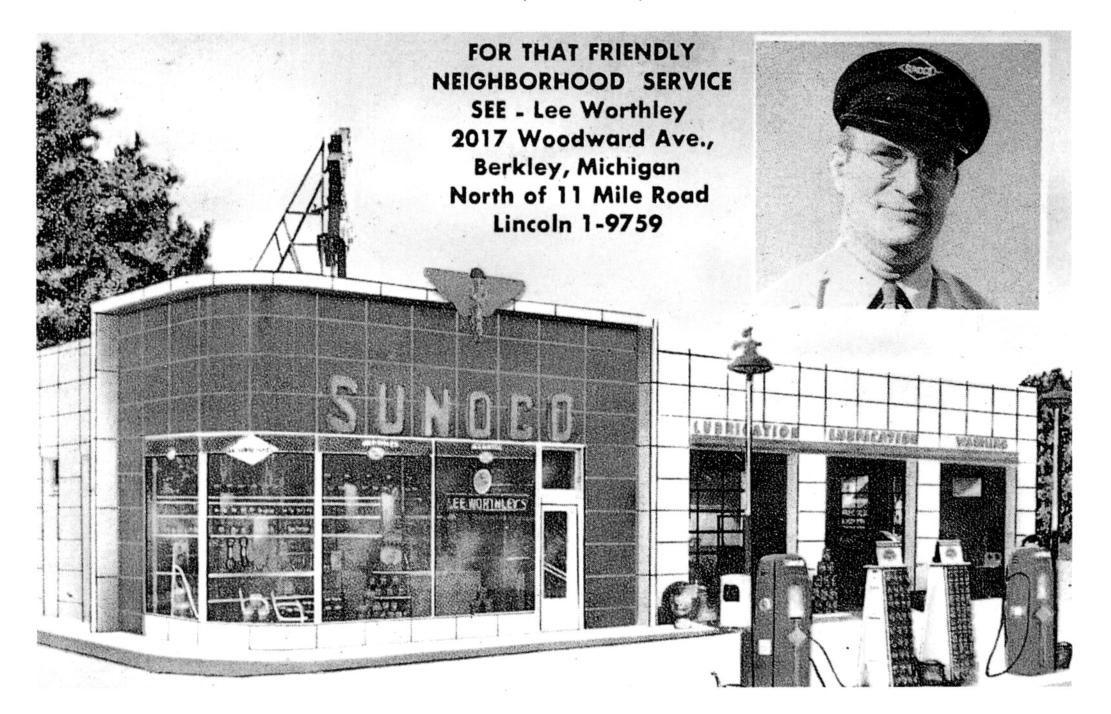

Gas station owner Lee Worthley was so proud of his neighborhood porcelain enamel gas station in Berkley, Michigan, that he had his own portrait prominently displayed on the postcard he had made in the 1950s. Sunoco's blue and yellow color scheme was enhanced by the caduceus borrowed from Saint Luke to enhance this vintage of Sun Oil Company designs.

Bill Smart's Amoco station in Magnolia, Arkansas, shines brightly at roadside with its curved corners emphasized by red racing stripes.

Moderne styling became all the rage in Cimarron, Kansas, when this Co-Op station was built in 1948. Even though the tile was still in good shape, it was recently painted over in off-white, and a new metal sign was attached to the tower to give the building a "more contemporary" appearance.

76
UNIO
SPARKLE CORPS
SPARKLE CORPS
SERVICE
STATION
INSPECTION
76
UNION
Safe • Clean

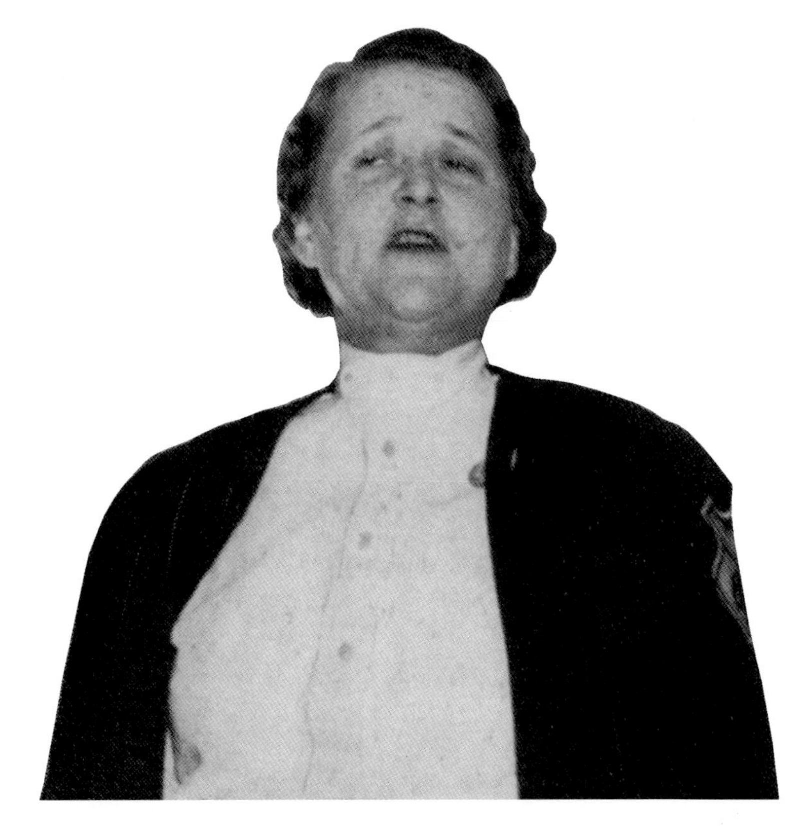

Phillips 66 launched its "Clean Rest Room Crusade" in 1938 by dispatching corps of Highway Hostesses in their sales areas. The Crusades were introduced by ceremonies in several cities, sometimes presided over by Mrs. Matilda Passmore, above, a "registered nurse, widely known traveler, and nationally known health lecturer," who reportedly "stressed the need for daily use of an approved germicide such as Lysol to overcome the inherent fear of women for possible disease which may be contracted in contact with unkept toilet fixtures." To further stress the importance of this program, Phillips 66 in 1939 issued a dealer booklet entitled "A Challenge Beyond Evasion."

REST ROOMS

Throughout the remainder of the teens and into the 1920s, the rest room became an essential service in nearly every gas station. Sometimes it was real plumbing inside, and other times an outhouse out back. By 1929, the humble john had evolved to the point where, in a luxurious SOHIO super service station in Cleveland, the ladies' lavatory was much more than that: "The ladies' rest room next to the lubritorium is a work of art in itself. Several mahogany chairs, a mahogany Period desk, and a Venetian wall mirror make up the delightful appointments of this room. Through a large plate glass window which opens on the lubritorium the woman driver may watch every operation that her car undergoes." The plumbing fixtures themselves must have been located in an antechamber.

But what for the most part had only been a passing interest in the lowly gas station toilet exploded into a frenzy of promotional activity in the mid-1930s. And this flood of attention was caused, no doubt, by the fact that many such facilities were Black Holes of Calcutta at best.

A dedicated and conscientious Texaco dealer emerges after performing the unenviable task of cleaning up his "Registered Rest Rooms."

In the 1930s oil companies targeted nearly all of their rest room promotions toward their women customers. In this magazine add for Shell's "Home-Clean" facilities, a woman's club official, without compensation, endorsed Shell's "White Cross of Cleanliness."

Texaco's Registered Rest Room Program was surely the industry leader in rest room promotion. "My 'powder room' on every road," proclaimed one billboard depicting a chic woman — powder puff in hand. Thousands of rest rooms were registered by number, and dealers took an eight-point pledge to keep their facilities clean and fully equipped. The pledge was posted on the bathroom wall, and outside at the curb was the familiar green-and-white Registered Rest Room sign. "The White Patrol," inspectors in a fleet of forty-eight two-door white coupes, crisscrossed the country to enforce the pledge.

REST ROOMS

Less well known, but even more fervent, was the Highway Hostess Program introduced by Phillips 66 late in 1938. Uniformed nurses cruised Phillips 66 territories in cream-and-green Plymouths, inspecting "Hospital Clean" facilities with a "Certified Rest Room" sign displayed in front of the station. Breathless rhetoric proclaimed the role of these latter-day Florence Nightingales: "Undaunted by heat waves, detours, and varied travel hardships these couriers of hospitality carry on continuously, in their sincere efforts to promote public hygiene and travel comfort to a greater degree than ever undertaken by service station sponsorship."

The Highway Hostesses, in addition to inspecting rest rooms, provided emergency first aid, helped "travel worn" mothers change diapers, and gave out ice water to stranded motorists. In 1939 the Hostesses visited each station an average of once a year, and this was increased to monthly visits in 1940. And this meant winter uniforms: "[The Highway Hostesses] are now smartly turned out in dawn-blue serge tailored suits, made very similar to those of the air-liner stewardess, but with an action-back for the jacket that gives driving freedom. For warmth, a navy blue serge cape, lined with a brilliant red of the same material, buttons onto the jacket lapels, and makes Miss Hostess about the smartest thing you ever saw."

Texaco's "Registered Rest Room," launched in the 1930s, was the best known and most widely promoted campaign of its type. Thousands of bathrooms were registered by number, and fleets of inspectors in little white coupes, as seen in this 1938 *Collier's* magazine advertisement, toured the country to make sure everything was spick and span.

FITTS & STARTS by STORM

WONDER WHY FOLKS DRIVIN' THROUGH ALWAYS HEAD FOR THAT **TEXACO** STATION?? WHAT'VE THEY GOT THAT WE HAVEN'T GOT??

HERE COMES JUDGE ROCKJAW.... HE GETS AROUND A LOT. ....ASK HIM!

FLATS FIXED

GUMBO OIL

IN THE FIRST PLACE, SAM, THEY MAINTAIN MODERN REST ROOMS AND THEY KEEP 'EM TIDY!!....THEY'RE CALLED **REGISTERED REST ROOMS!!**

I DON'T BELIEVE IN CODDLIN' THE PUBLIC, BUT WE'LL FIGHT FIRE WITH FIRE, PLUTO!...... TAKE THE MOP AN' PAIL, AND TIDY THE REST ROOM WHILST I FIX A SIGN!!

REGISTERED REST ROOMS, MY EYE! **WE'LL GO 'EM ONE BETTER!**

GUESS THAT'LL HOLD 'EM!

YOU DON'T HAVE TO **REGISTER** HERE!! **COME RIGHT IN!**

Texaco was not above poking fun at itself and its program, as witnessed by this 1947 comic from its own *Texaco Dealer* magazine.

The message is smarmy but clear in this advertising illustration that appeared in a 1938 issue of *Life* magazine.

Although the Phillips 66 program was ended with the onset of World War II, Texaco's Registered Rest Room Program, after a wartime break, continued onward, as did rest room mania in general. Esso gave out "Comfort Awards." A Union Oil gas station in Pasadena, California, designed in 1949 by Raymond Loewy, offered foot-pedal control of water facilities for "new heights of sanitation and convenience."

The last gasp of the "inspector" phenomenon may have been Union Oil's Sparkle Corps of the late 1950s and early 1960s, supporting the company's avowed belief that "cleanliness is next to godliness."

Women in stewardess-like uniforms and white gloves —"models, secretaries, recent college grads"— would spend the summer traveling from rest room to rest room. The company's magazine informs us that Sparkle Girls had ridden in parades, appeared in movies, and had even been pressed into service as gas pumpers. And Sparkle Girl Mary McLeod's life was changed forever as she walked out of a men's room and right into a "tall handsome marine lieutenant" named Levalle. Mary won't be a Sparkle Girl this year, we are told, because "she's too busy being a housewife."

The public rest room is every bit as important to a gas station business today as it ever was. Behind locked doors, often emblazoned with the admonition "Customers Only," are found the plumbing fixtures of necessity. Most convenience stores also provide these facilities, although the motorist sometimes has to go into the back room behind the refrigerator cases to get to them. And sometimes these bathrooms are clean and well supplied. Although the hullabaloo has disappeared, the basic needs remain the same.

This heavy metal Shell badge, a highly valued artifact, probably graced a gas attendant's cap in the 1930s.

A jolly advertising thermometer given away by a garage in Pennsylvania in the 1930s captures all of the hubbub, glamour, and romance of the gas station experience.

THE BEST OF THE BEST

RAZZMATAZZ

Today, an entire organized subculture collects, buys, sells, trades, and covets "petroliana": gas globes, oil cans, signs, road maps, postcards, toys, and myriad other ephemeral evidence. When a bunch of dealers set up together, it isn't a flea market, it's a "gas bash." There's a national gasfest at a motel near the Des Moines, Iowa, airport every summer. Peter Capell, an otherwise sane man who lives near Chicago, has a collection of 78 different sets of plastic gas pump–shaped salt and pepper shakers. Jim Masson, who lives near Kansas City, has more than 15,000 road maps. Crazed gasaholics haunt garage and yard sales to try to nab a precious something. Nostalgic memories and predatory instincts run hand in hand.

The hobby of collecting gas station memorabilia is fast becoming more popular. Prices are going up. The good stuff is getting harder and harder to find. And so it goes.

NOVEMBER

SUN	MON	TUE	WED	THU	FRI	SAT
1	2	3	4	5	6	7
8	9	10	11	12	13	14
15	16	17	18	19	20	21
22	23	24	25	26	27	28
29	30					

December 1959

JANUARY

SUN	MON	TUE	WED	THU	FRI	SAT
					1	2
3	4	5	6	7	8	9
10	11	12	13	14	15	16
17	18	19	20	21	22	23
24/31	25	26	27	28	29	30

First Quarter 7
Full Moon 15
Last Quarter 23
New Moon 29

SUNDAY	MONDAY	TUESDAY	WEDNESDAY	THURSDAY	FRIDAY	SATURDAY
		1	2	3	4	5
6	7	8	9	10	11	12
13	14	15	16	17	18	19
20	21	22	23	24	25	26
27	28	29	30	31		

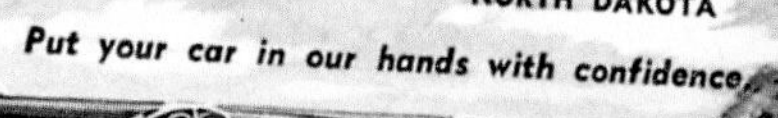

HAPPY NEW YEAR

MARSLAND STANDARD SERVICE
PHONE: 59-137
Corner 4th Ave. & 5th St. S. E.
MINOT NORTH DAKOTA
Put your car in our hands with confidence

Standard Oil of Indiana couldn't have realized the irony of the opening image of its 1960 gift calendar. A ski-jumping innocent babe, proudly bearing the Standard Gold and Red Crowns, plummets into the new decade, the decade in which these crowns would disappear from the tops of pumps and when much of the fun would disappear entirely from petroleum promotion and marketing.

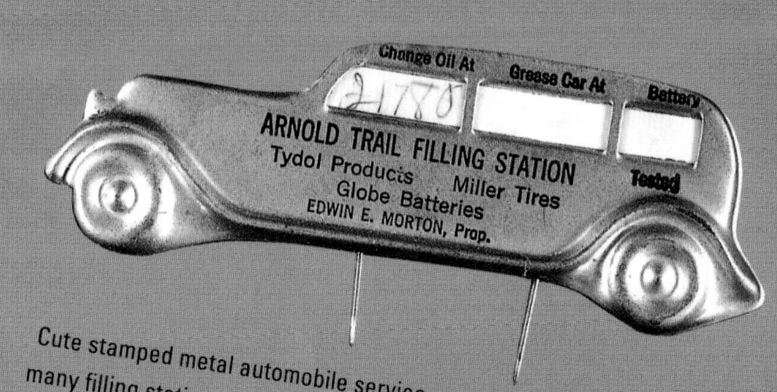

Cute stamped metal automobile service reminders were given away by many filling stations in the 1930s so that they could be pinned on the sun visor to encourage return visits.

A NARROW SQUEAK!
BUT WE MADE IT...
THANKS TO ATLANTIC WHITE FLASH PLUS
ATLANTIC WHITE FLASH PLUS–PICK-UP!

In 1934, the Atlantic Refining Company gave away small comic booklets featuring their "3 Little Men"—"White," "Flash," and "Plus," named, fittingly enough, after their own brand of premium gasoline.

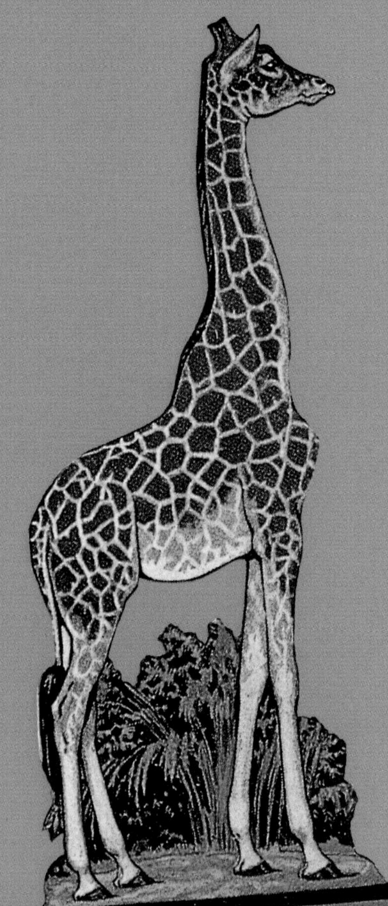

HEAD & SHOULDERS
ABOVE THEM ALL
BETHOLINE

FOLD BACK

FOLD BACK

FOLD UNDER

NOTHING ELSE
LIKE IT!
BETHOLINE

FOLD BACK

FOLD BACK

FOLD UNDER

The A. F. Gilmore Gas Company, based in Los Angeles, was known for its colorful promotional gimmicks. The 1935 Gilmore road map is highly sought after by collectors because of its outstanding, brilliantly produced graphic design.

Betholine, " The Wonder Motor Fuel," gave out a series of ten cutout animal cards to kids in the 1930s, including the two shown here, and Folger McKinsey, "The Betholine Bard," wrote an appropriate poem on the back of each card, including:

A gentle creature, the Giraffe,
But at him you will always laugh,
He is so tall, his head so high,
And there's a twinkle in his eye.

That twinkle is because he knows
He's head and shoulder over those
Who envy him — like men with gas
When Betholine says: "Let me pass!"

In the 1920s, the Jenney Gasoline Company gave out decks of cards with their attractive colonial-style stations depicted on one side. The cards were cleverly packaged in four-way slipcases, which were used to take from table to table in duplicate bridge tournaments.

CHAPTER 5

BACK TO THE FUTURE: 1965–1990

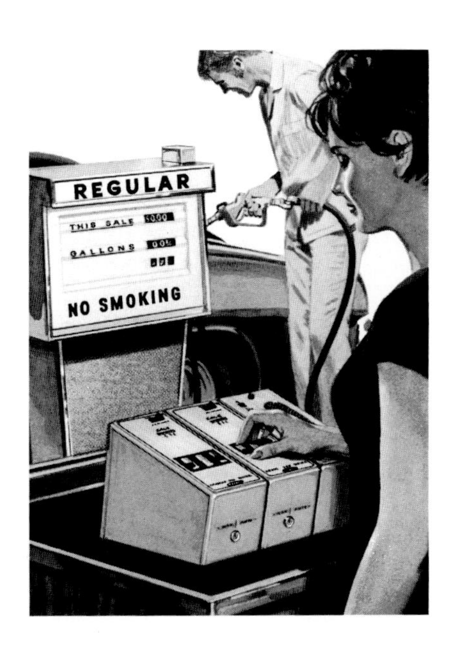

The history of gas stations and petroleum marketing in the last quarter of this century has been much like that of many once proud and individualistic enterprises. The traditional service station has been replaced by much more efficient but anonymous-looking facilities. And during this evolution of necessity, the selling of gasoline lost its heart and soul and all of its pizzazz.

The beginning of the end was already in sight when the interstate highway system, a plan and a dream in the 1950s, became the increasingly dominant homogenizing force in the landscape of the 1960s. In the middle 1960s, the so-called highway beautification movement, spearheaded by well-intentioned people like Ladybird Johnson, threatened all commercial razzle-dazzle and honky-tonk by denouncing it as visual pollution.

Since the new interstate highway bypassed the old commercial strips, it doomed them to obscurity and economic starvation. The final blows to the traditional gas station were the gas shortages of 1973 and 1979, directly caused by the Arab oil embargo and the Iranian revolution. Gas prices skyrocketed and tempers flared in long gas lines.

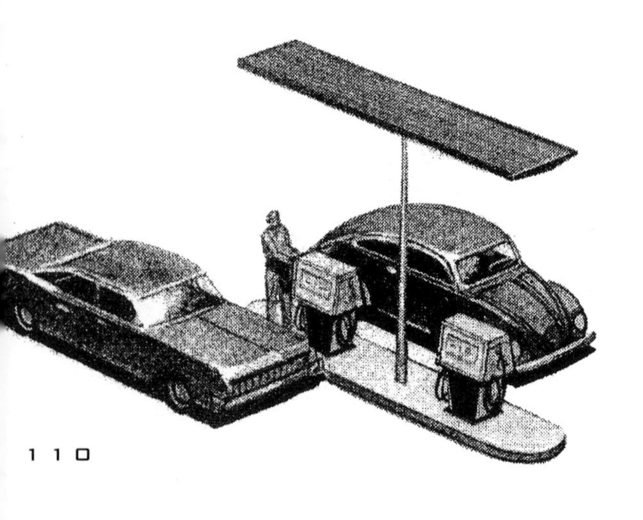

An old station stands deserted on Highway 89 in Wilhoit, Arizona, with the two pumps standing out front as anachronistic as the station itself. The new reality, above, is remotely operated, prepay, self-service pumps as illustrated in a Tokheim Corporation brochure.

BRAKES
CLOSED

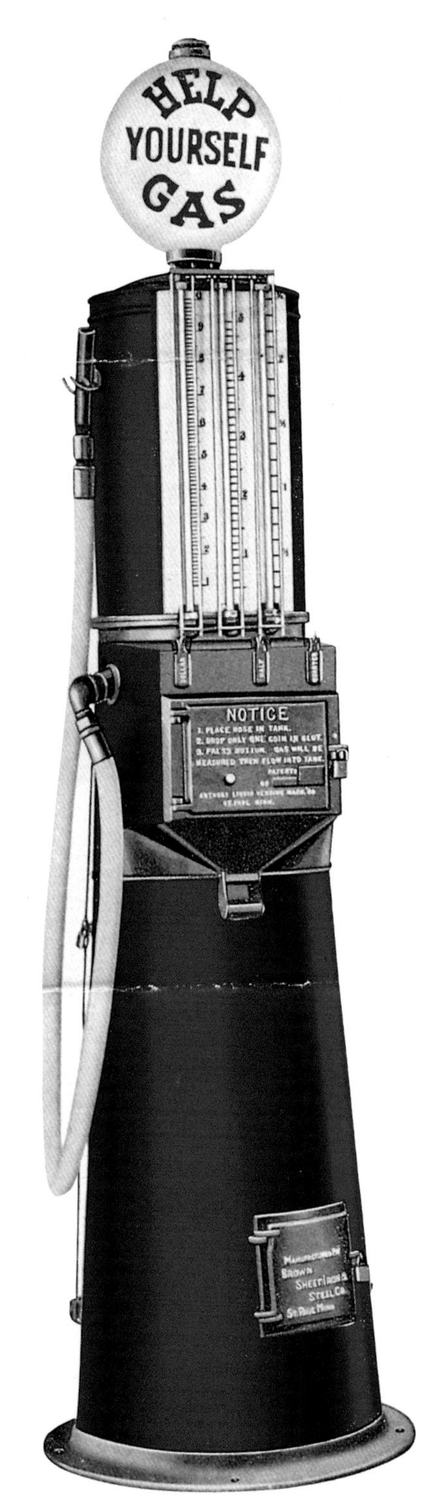

Surprisingly, the self-service phenomenon in gasoline marketing dates from as early as the 1920s, as witnessed by "The Anthony," a 24-hour "automatic salesman."

The first wave of self-serve economy gas stations were to be found in southern California in the late 1940s. This Gilmore outlet in Los Angeles featured endless rows of pumps, and the motorists willing to do it themselves got smelly dirty hands and a savings of merely five cents a gallon.

Out on the new highways, the speed limit was reduced to 55 miles per hour. Getting there — getting anywhere — was no longer half the fun. It was nearly no fun at all. A tourist's drive, once a meandering adventure, became endless ribbons of two-, three-, and four-lane highways. No billboards. Fenced-off right-of-ways. EZ on — EZ offs.

The new structures built to serve hypnotized motorists were equally homogenized. "Interstate Cities" sprang up in the middle of nowhere beside off-ramps, each remarkable only in its nearly identical appearance to the one that came before and the one that would inevitably come next. The buildings along these universal strips were standardized and franchised — Holiday Inns, McDonald's, IHOPs — and the new gas stations were super self-serves and pumps in front of convenience stores.

Self-service pumps didn't really begin to catch on until the late 1940s, although there were coin-operated gas pump designs dating from the 1920s. Whether they were just pipe dreams, or if somewhere someone actually built and used them, is another matter. One such device was "The Anthony," proclaimed in a brochure put out by the Anthony Liquid Vending Machine Company in Saint Paul, Minnesota. "An automatic salesman, as well as a service machine," The Anthony was touted as the "greatest pump of the age," an "automatic vending machine," and a "24 hour service station."

But a man named Frank Urich, who opened his first gas station in Los Angeles in May 1947, with much fanfare and girls on roller skates collecting gas money from consumers, is credited as the founder of self-service marketing operations. By cutting frills and labor costs, he cut a few cents per gallon from the retail price of gas.

It is reported by an acquaintance of Mr. Urich that he got the idea for self-service while standing in a cafeteria line: "He noticed that people going through the line put more food on their trays than they would

Mobil Oil hired architects Elliot Noyes and graphic designers Chermayeff & Geismar Associates as white knights to revitalize their roadside image. The result was a stark but elegant station design and a gracefully recast Flying Red Horse on a white disc. Noyes's brushed-aluminum casing for the gas pumps was high industrial art of the first order.

The predominant trend in gas station design in the 1960s and '70s was conservative dullness. This 1967 Mobil station design was intended to blend into suburban ranch house environments with its rustic brick and phony cupola.

ordinarily when they sat down and ordered. He thought they might do the same thing at self-service gas pumps." Urich was right, at least for a while.

But the idea of self-service really caught on with a vengeance after the gas shortage of 1973–1974. In 1969 only 16 percent of gas was sold self-serve, a figure that rose to 35 percent by 1975, 72 percent by 1982, and 80 percent by 1987. The new self-serves evolved after the introduction of remote-control, automated pumps perfected by the mid-1960s. At this time, because of safety considerations, self-service was legal in only thirteen states. By 1981, all but two states (New Jersey and Oregon) had legalized this practice.

Convenience stores are said to date from 1927, when a manager of the Southland Ice Company in Dallas decided to stock a few grocery items to attract winter business. Southland is the same corporation that developed the archetypal model for all convenience stores — the 7-Eleven. In the early 1970s, some convenience stores put pumps out front to attract customers into their stores. But the gas, by itself, also proved to be profitable.

At the pinnacle of the Southland's convenience store–gas station marketing arrangement in the 1970s, nearly one-half of the 8,000 7-Eleven stores were selling gas — a total of two billion gallons a year. But in the early 1980s, convenience stores began to develop financial problems. And the major oil companies, knowing a good thing when they saw it, began to develop their own convenience stores beside their pumps.

The monumental and ornamental gas station at the Madonna Inn complex in San Luis Obispo, California, completed in 1968, is a throwback to the good old days. The station is built of enormous boulders, the largest being some fifteen to twenty tons, and the office is topped by a spire decorated by inner-lit floral plastic panels.

In the 1980s Texaco hired the design firm Anspach Grossman Portugal to add some zip to their roadside image, and the resulting matte black and bright red modular design gave a handsome and assertive identity to new convenience stores and self-serves.

Even before the dominance of self-service and convenience stores, the new architecture of gasoline responded in a variety of ways to the new demands of the modern age. In response to the "ugliness" complaints of the beautification movement of the 1960s, many oil companies remodeled their stations to make them more "attractive." Texaco added plastic stone siding and mansard roofs, and the once proud Texaco star was reduced to a red asterisk. Companies like Amoco and Sunoco "colonialized" their stations, adding phony rafters to old flat roofs, sometimes with a phony cupola plunked on the peak.

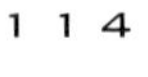

The gas station canopy, which had been growing in size and shape since the 1940s, became nearly the entire architectural expression of the high-volume, self-service gas stations. Huge canopies covering most of the site would protect the many pump islands. And a tiny little building, sometimes just a booth protected by bulletproof glass with one person inside — like a bank teller — to operate the automated pumps and collect money, nestled under the canopy. Or sometimes the building wasn't so tiny, but a small convenience store additionally selling grocery items and convenience foods.

But not all of this architecture was awful and anonymous. And most of it was carefully and efficiently planned to serve its purposes.

Mobil Oil took the strong step of hiring Elliot Noyes to redesign their corporate image in the 1960s. Noyes, an architect and designer of great talent and elegance, worked with graphic designers Chermayeff & Geismar Associates and produced a prototype building — a sparse but clear modern design of brick and stone with an umbrella-shaped canopy above the pumps. The pumps themselves became objects of high industrial art, sheathed in their Noyes-designed brushed aluminum casing.

Texaco hired strong designers to clean up their image in the early 1980s. The New York design firm Anspach Grossman Portugal, and specifically designer Ken Love, came up with the "System 2000" for Texaco. The "system" was used to construct very handsome

Texaco tried to keep up with the times in the far-out late 1960s, and the corporation considered coordinated casual uniform designs for women including hot pants and miniskirts, but these ideas got no further than the drafting board.

self-serves and convenience stores, made more distinctive by their matte black finish. System 2000 also marked the reappearance of a strong Texaco Star as the corporate symbol.

The beginning of the end was inevitable for the traditional service station. The statistical evidence is clear. In 1972, there were still 226,459 service stations in operation. But by 1990, there were only 111,657, a drop of 51 percent. While there were 135,000 gas stations in the repair business in 1978, that number had plummeted to 59,000 by 1987.

There were numerous reasons for this fall from grace. After the gas shortages of the 1970s, many of the older stations were deactivated. Gas consumption itself dropped slowly during several years in the '70s. The newer models and makes of cars required much less maintenance, and specialized repair businesses, places like Midas Muffler and Jiffy Lubes, were able to undercut the price of repairs and service at gas stations.

Some old gas pumps died, while others just faded away. A trio of Olympic pumps in El Cajon, California, and a pair of Atlantic pumps in Sloansville, New York, anthropomorphic creatures all, with their hoses draped across their chests, seem to be reciting an elegiac pledge of allegiance.

An old Gulf Disc barely clinging to life on Main Street in Walsenburg, Colorado, has through weathering and juxtaposition become an ad hoc example of abstract art that might otherwise be found in a modern art museum.

The final nails in the coffin have come as a result of the new environmental regulations in the 1980s. Station owners had to assume responsibility, through expensive liability insurance, to protect the groundwater beneath storage tanks; the storage tanks themselves had to be replaced; and additional expenses were incurred, including new underground piping to accommodate the new vapor recovery nozzles.

It's a wonder, therefore, that any full-service gas stations remain in business today. They're few and far between, and the attrition rate is ever increasing. And that raises the question of what to do with the old

buildings, some of which were quite splendid edifices built with style for their mundane but important function. Sadly, many have been deserted and stand on the back roads bypassed by the interstates — decaying monuments to the romantic era of petroleum. Others, in more fortuitous locations, have undergone drastic "renovations" to become high-volume, self-service "super pumpers," with little or no resemblance to their former appearances.

But many other old gas stations, with their pumps removed, have gone on to lead a wide variety of new lives. Some have been converted to residential use. There was a gas station church in the San Fernando Valley of Los Angeles. Other uses are endless, varied, and at least ecologically correct: gift shops, beauty shops, pet stores, real estate offices, bars, restaurants, and so on.

These rescued relics will soon, no doubt, be the only physical evidence of a vibrant tradition in twentieth-century American culture, glorious little shells that once housed grease and grime, sweat and toil; sparkling, and sometimes not-so-sparkling, rest rooms; hydraulic lifts and grease pits; sales areas for tires, batteries, and accessories; and racks of free road maps for future adventures.

Outside were grand totemic pumps with innerlit globes; porcelain enamel signs displaying some of the great commercial graphic symbols of our age; and bunting and strings of pennants flapping in the wind.

Now that the era of the small neighborhood gas station has come and gone, the old buildings have sometimes gone on to lead new lives. A porcelain enamel station in Pacoima, California, became a church with its painted sign in the parking lot. In Trinidad, Colorado, an adobe mission-style outlet was revived as a pet-grooming salon. And in Harlingen, Texas, a wild and crazy little station was about to come back to life as a taco stand.

Gone are the days when gas stations would brag of being "the most beautiful" in the state and when guys named Mack, Pep, Polly, and Danie in their distinctive and handsome tall peaked caps would rush out to meet, greet, and serve customers.

And, scurrying in and out, in spiffy uniforms and caps bedecked with patches and badges, were the gas station owners and employees themselves — the backbone of a tradition of the small businessman in our free-enterprise system.

But all of this is gone now, and we won't see the likes of it again. Individualism has been replaced by computerized predictability. Small businesses have been swallowed up and digested by franchised, corporate monoliths.

The cultural and functional phenomenon that began as a pump in front of a grocery store in the early twentieth century has been replaced by pumps in front of convenience stores. The gas station has come full circle in its short but vivid and fascinating history. And, as they say, what goes around, comes around. We're back to the future.

Goodrich
TEXACO
ETHYL
Refiners
TEXACO
Refiners
Refiners
TEXACO

GAS
LAST CHANCE
GAS
GAS
OIL

Acknowledgments

THANKS TO: Terry Hackford, my antiknock editor; Eric Baker and Kai Zimmermann, for their high octane book design; and Mike Mattil, my copyeditor, for his great tune-up; Kevin Holloway at the library of the American Petroleum Institute, for research help above and beyond the call of duty; Mike Pniewski, for his generosity and help in loaning his collection of petroleum-related items; Andreas Brown, for his vision and guidance; Doug Yorke, for sharing his knowledge and enthusiasm about road maps; Peter Ledwith, for his help with research matters, and his knowledge of Canadian oil companies; and to Richard Miller, for sharing his premier collection of hand-tinted photographs and his time and interest in getting them to me.

Those organizations and individuals who helped to sponsor and underwrite the cost of the photography: The Architectural League of New York; Tom Bailey; Susan Butler; Asher Edelman; Rosalie Genevro; the Howard Gilman Foundation; Toni Greenberg; the John Simon Guggenheim Memorial Foundation; Agnes Gund; Ellen Harris; Barbara Jakobson; Philip Johnson; Rick Landau; the Sidney and Francis Lewis Foundation; Jim McClure; the Design Arts and Visual Arts Programs of the National Endowment for the Arts in Washington, D.C., a federal agency; the New York Foundation for the Arts; Harold Ramis; and Virginia Wright.

The helpful and friendly people at the oil and gas pump companies who assisted with the research and contributed visual materials: Felicia Bagby and Walter A. Coyne at the Atlantic Richfield Company; Susan Box and Rob Phillips at the Phillips Petroleum Company; Rob Burns at the Dresser-Wayne Pump Company; Marjorie Federici and Diane Mansfield at Texaco, Inc.; Pat Hill at the Sun Oil Company; Hank Hilty at the A. F. Gilmore Company; Dorothy Jankowski at BP America, Inc.; Mary C. Keane at the Mobil Corporation; Maureen A. Kenney, Laurie R. Sachtleben, and Marie Tilson at the Chevron Corporation; Carolyn Killebrew at the Exxon Company U. S. A.; Paul E. Lamoureux at Gilbarco, Inc.; Tom Pardo at the Amoco Corporation; Barbara Pederson at the Unocal Corporation; Dillon Scott at the Shell Oil Company; Rollie Smith and Shirley Stewart at the Marathon Oil Company; Mike Tanyard at the Tokheim Pump Company; Shel Vedlitz at Conoco, Inc.; Stephen M. Wright at OXY USA INC.; and Kent Young at CITGO.

Those individuals and organization who gave access to their private collections of historical materials: Andreas Brown at the Gotham Book Mart; Peter Capell; Alan Goldberg at AG/ENA; Jim Heimann; Carolyn Kozo at the Security Pacific Historical Photograph Collection at the Los Angeles Public Library; Gary Kuritz at the California State Library Photo Collection; Peter M. Ledwith; Ernest Malcom; Jim Masson; Dottie McKenna at the American Petroleum Institute; Richard Miller; Rich Musante; Don and Newly Preziosi; Leonard Schechter at Urban Archaeology; Roger Steckler; Billie Stiff; C. A. Taubert; Ione Wommack; Doug Yorke; and Tom Zimmerman.

To the individuals and institutions which gave of their time, knowledge and resources in the preparation of this book: Billy and Janice Adler; Charles Anderson; Barbara Anthony at the Randolph County Chamber of Commerce, Roanoke, Alabama; Lewis Baer; Barbara Barnhill-West at the Museum of East Alabama; Dave Cole; Ruth Collings; John Deforest; Stan De Orsey; David Farmer at the DeGolyer Library, Southern Methodist University; David Gebhard; Bob Goodyear; Emily Gwathmey; Michael Kaplan; Dan Kirchner at the Motor Vehicle Manufacturers Association; Bob Lee; Roger LeRoque; Noel Levy; Ed Love; Ken Love at Anspach Grossman Portugal; Marshall Lumsden; Patsy Madden at Chermayeff & Geismar Associates; Alex and Phyllis Madonna; Charlie Middleton; Dick Mitchell; Leland and Crystal Payton; Bev Powers at the University Archives, Auburn University; Beth L. Savage at the National Register of Historic Places; Karen Shatzkin; Becky Shiffer; Craig Solomonson; Tim Thompson and Roger B. White at the Division of Transportation, National Museum of American History, at the Smithsonian Institution; Tom Todd; Susan Tunick; Michael and Marion Usher; Cynthia Van Hazinga; and Fred and Barb Volkman.

SELECTED BIBLIOGRAPHY

BOOKS

Andrews, J. J. C. The Well-Built Elephant and Other Roadside Attractions: A Tribute to American Eccentricity. Congdon & Weed, 1984.

Anderson, Robert O. *Fundamentals of the Petroleum Industry.* University of Oklahoma Press, 1984.

Anderson, Scott. *Check the Oil: A Pictorial History of the American Filling Station (Gas Station Collectibles with Prices).* Wallace-Homestead Book Company, 1986.

Anderson Warren H. *Vanishing Roadside America.* University of Arizona Press, 1981.

Anderson, Will. *Mid-Atlantic Roadside Delights.* Anderson & Sons' Publishing Company, 1991.

———. *New England Roadside Delights.* Will Anderson Publisher, 1989.

Ansaldi, *Richard. Souvenirs from the Roadside West.* Harmony Books, 1978.

Ant Farm. *Automerica: A Trip down U.S. Highways from World War II to the Future.* E. P. Dutton & Company, 1976.

Automobile Club of America. *Tour Book.* Automobile Club of America, 1911.

Baeder, John. *Gas, Food and Lodging.* Abbeville Press, 1982.

Baker, Eric, and Tyler Blik. *Trademarks of the 20's and 30's.* Chronicle Books, 1986.

———. *Trademarks of the 40's and 50's.* Chronicle Books, 1986.

Baker, Eric, and Jane Martin. *Great Inventions, Good Intentions: An Illustrated History of Design Patents.* Chronicle Books, 1990.

Beaton, Kendall. *Enterprise in Oil: A History of Shell in the United States.* Appleton-Century-Crofts, 1957.

Blake, Peter. *God's Own Junkyard: The Planned Deterioration of America's Landscape,* New and Updated. Holt, Rinehart and Winston, 1964, 1979.

Drivas, Larry T., and J. Peterson Powell. *Gas and Oil Trademarks.* Villa Publishing Syndicate, 1992.

Ellis, William Donahue. *On the Oil Lands with Cities Service.* Cities Service Oil and Gas Corporation, 1983.

Gasoline Pump Manufacturers Association (compilers). *Gasoline Pump Blue Book,* First, Second and Third Editions, 1927–1941, 1942–1947 and 1947–1952.

Gebhard, David, and Harriette Von Breton. *Los Angeles in the Thirties: 1931–1941,* Second Edition, Revised and Enlarged. Hennessey & Ingalls, 1975, 1989.

Giddens, Paul E. *Standard Oil Company (Indiana): Oil Pioneer of the Middle West.* Appleton-Century-Crofts, 1955.

Giebelhaus, August W. *Business and Government in the Oil Industry: A Case Study of Sun Oil, 1876–1945.* JAI Press, 1947.

Harding, R. Brewster. *Roadside New England 1900–1955: A photgraphic postcard record of the Eastern Illustrating & Publishing Company of Belfast, Maine.* Old Port Publishing Company, 1982.

Heimann, Jim, and Rip Georges. *California Crazy: Roadside Vernacular Architecture.* Chronicle Books, 1980.

Jackson, John Brinckerhoff. *Discovering the Vernacular Landscape.* Yale University Press, 1984.

Jackson, J. B. *Landscapes.* University of Massachusetts Press, 1970.

———. *The Necessity for Ruins and Other Topics.* University of Massachusetts Press, 1980.

Jakle, John A. *The Tourist: Travel in Twentieth Century North America.* University of Nebraska Press, 1985.

James, Marquis. *The Texaco Story: The First Fifty Years 1902–1952.* Texas Company, 1953.

Jennings, Jan (editor). *Roadside America: The Automobile in Design and Culture.* Iowa State University Press for the Society for Commercial Archeology, 1990.

Jones, Charles S. *From the Rio Grande to the Arctic: The Story of the Richfield Oil Corporation.* University of Oklahoma Press, 1972.

Keller, Ulrich. *The Highway as Habitat: A Roy Stryker Documentation, 1943–1955.* University Art Museum, Santa Barbara, California, 1986.

Liebs, Chester H. *Main Street to Miracle Mile: American Roadside Architecture.* A New York Graphic Society Book/ Little, Brown & Company, 1985.

Lee, Bob. *Gilbert & Barker Gilbarco, Inc: A Pictorial History of the Growth of a Great Company.* Harlo Press, 1989.

———. *S. F. Bowser & Co., Incorporated,* volume I. Harlo Press, 1978.

———. *10 Gallons for a Dollar: A Pictorial History of Gas Pump Companies and Service Stations.* Harlo Press, 1985.

———. *Tokheim Pump Company, Ft. Wayne, Indiana: An Illustrated History, 1901–1980.* Harlo Press, 1980.

Love, Ed. *Gas and Oil Trademarks,* volume 2. Villa Publishing Syndicate

Love, Ed, and Larry T. Drivas. *Gas and Oil Trademarks,* volume I. Villa Publishing Syndicate, 1988.

———. *Gas Stations and Related Designs: United States Design Patents Series One,* volumes 2,3 and 4. Villa Publishing Syndicate, 1990, 1990 and 1992.

McCabe, Axe, and Ed Love. *Gas Stations and Related Designs: United States Design Patents Series One,* volume I. Villa Publishing Syndicate, 1989.

Margolies, John. *The End of the Road: Vanishing Highway Architecture in America.* Penguin Books in Collaboration with the Hudson River Museum, 1977, 1978, 1981.

Morgan, Hal. *Symbols of America: A Lavish Celebration of America's Best-Loved Trademarks and the Products They Symbolize—Their History, Folklore and Enduring Mystique.* A Steam Press Book, Penguin Books, 1986.

Partridge, Bellamy. *Fill'er Up!: The Story of Fifty Years of Motoring.* McGraw-Hill, 1952.

Pedersen, Barbara L. *Unocal 1890–1990: A Century of Spirit,* Unocal Corporation, 1990.

Ruscha, Edward. *Twenty-six Gasoline Stations.* Cunningham Press, 1967, 1969.

Sampson, Anthony. *The Seven Sisters: The Great Oil Companies and the World They Made.* Hodder and Stoughton, 1975.

Sears, Stephen W. *The American Heritage History of the Automobile in America.* American Heritage Publishing Company, 1977.

Spence, Hartzell (editorial consultant). *A Great Name in Oil: Sinclair Through Fifty Years.* F. W. Dodge Company/ McGraw-Hill, 1966.

Sun Oil Company. *Centennial Celebration: The Story of Sun Company.* Sun Oil Company, 1986.

Taylor, Frank J., and Earl W. Welty. *Sign of the 76: The Fabulous Life and Times of the Union Oil Company of California.* Union Oil Company of California, 1976.

Venturi, Robert, Denise Scott Brown, and Steven Izenour. *Learning from Las Vegas,* revised edition. MIT Press, 1977, 1972.

Vieyra, Daniel I. *"Fill 'er Up": An Architectural History of America's Gas Stations.* Collier Books, 1979.

Wertz, William C. (editor). *Phillips—The First 66 Years.* Phillips Petroleum Company, 1983.

Williamson, Harold F., Ralph L. Andreano, Arnold R. Daum, and Gilbert C.Klose. *The American Peroleum Industry: The Age of Energy, 1899–1959.* Northwestern University Press, 1963.

Yergin, Daniel. *The Prize: The Epic Quest for Oil, Money and Power.* Simon & Schuster, 1991.

PERIODICALS:

American Heritage "Sorry, No Gas: How Americans Met the First Great Gasoline Crisis — Nearly Forty Years Ago," by Stephen W. Sears, October/ November 1979, pp. 5–17.

American Petroleum Institute "The Decline of Gasoline Service Stations and Motorists' Access to Car Maintenance Services," Discussion Paper #058 by Thomas F. Hogarty, March 1989, 19 pp.

———. "Facts About Oil," July 1984, 44 pp.

———. "The Origin and Evolution of Gasoline Marketing," Research Study #022 by Thomas F. Hogarty, October 1, 1981, 79 pp.

Energy Information Administration. Office of Oil and Gas, U. S. Department of Energy, "The Motor Gasoline Industry: Past, Present and Future," January 1991, 56 pp.

Fortune. "The Wayne Pump Co.—Streamlined," August 1937, pp. 78–83 and 118–119.

Journal of American Culture. "The American Gasoline Station, 1920–1970", by John A. Jakle, Fall 1978, pp. 520–542.

Marathon World. "One Hundred Years on the Frontier (Marathon Oil Company), "special issue, Norman V. Richards (editor), 1988, 138 pp.

National Petroleum News, "History of Convenience Stores Linked to American Mobility," September 1990, pp. 63–72.

———. "How the Self–Serve Revolution Bred Price Wars and C–Stores," by Marvin Reid, February 1984, pp. 92–98.

———. "Money to be Made: The Oil–Marketing Story — A Quick History of Oil Marketing," 60th Anniversary issue, February 1969, pp. 111–134.

———. "Where Oil Got It's Trademarks," August 1959, pp.129, 131–132.

New York Sunday News Magazine. "Pump and Circumstance: The Romance of Our Old Gas Stations," by John Margolies, January 2, 1977, pp. 19–21 and 23.

The Oil Daily. "125 Years of Oil in America—1895–1900: 'Drake's Folly' Ignites Change," August 27, 1984, pp. 7–12.

———. "125 Years of Oil in America—1901–1930: The Modern Oil Industry Takes Shape," August 27, 1984, pp. 15–21.

———. "Past 25 Years Have Seen Major Changes in Marketing," by John R. Hahn, August 27, 1984, pp. 65 and 71.

———. "Winning Customers Is Always a Challenge: Gasoline Marketing's Colorful Tradition," by Susan L. Hahn, August 27, 1984, pp. 50–51.

Old Cars Weekly. "Gas Rationing During World War II, America Got Used to Walking Again," by Raymond Schuessler, September 16, 1982, pp. 18 and 22.

Service Station Management. "The Oil Industry 1859 to 1959 to ?: Highlights form the First Century," November 1959, pp. 40–41 and 72.

Sohio Sales Lab Notes. "The Sohio Story: A Brief History of Standard Oil, People and Progress, July 25, 1955, 28 pp.

The Sohioan. "75th Anniversary: The Standard Oil Company (Ohio)," special issue, January 10, 1945, 62 pp.

Special Interest Autos. "From Blacksmith's Shed to Lysicrates' Tomb," by Ray Scroggins, September/October 1975, pp. 27–31.

PERIODICALS-
GAS PUMPS:

Antique Automobile. "The Silent Sentinel of the American Road," Part I, January 1964, pp. 18–27, Part II, March 1964, pp. 24–32.

100 Years of Wayne. Wayne Division Dresser Industries, 1991, 32 pp.

S. F. Bowser & Company, Inc., Oil Tank and Pump Works, Ft. Wayne, Indiana. "Bulletins 2000–2800, Second Edition," 1913–1916.

PERIODICALS-
ROAD MAPS:

American Heritage. "Unfolding," by Ben Yagoda, April, 1988, pp. 34–41.

American Urban Guidenotes: The Newsletter of Guidebooks. "The Automobile Revolution," by John Fondersmith, volume 3, no. 1, September 1982, pp. 1–3.

The Lamp. "Getting from Here to There," by Ernest Dunbar, Fall 1983, pp. 12–15.

SCA Newsjournal. "Blazed Trails: Happy Motoring Across America the Beautiful," by Douglas Yorke, Jr., volume 11, no. 3, September 1982, pp. 1–3.

Scientific Monthly. "American Road Maps and Guides," by Walter W. Ristow, May, 1946, pp. 397–406.

Surveying and Mapping. "A Half Century of Oil–Company Road Maps," by Walter W. Ristow, volume 24, no. 4, December 1964, pp. 617–637.

PERIODICALS-
GENERAL PUBLICATIONS:

Check The Oil! Magazine, published by the International Petroliana Collectors Association, 2151 E. Dublin–Greenville Rd., #G–292, Columbus, Ohio 43229.

Garage Door News, Canadian Service Station Memorabilia Association, R. R. 4 Rockwood, Ontario NOB 2KO.

The Society for Commercial Archeology (SCA) NewsJournal, c/o Room 5010, National Museum of American History, Smithsonian Institution, Washington, D. C. 20506.

The Super Service Station, published by the Irving–Cloud Publishing Co., Chicago, IL., 1929–1987.

The Tiger Rag, The PoweRoyal Company (Villa Publishing Syndicate, Inc.), Box 25763, Colorado Springs, Co. 80936–5763.

OIL COMPANY MAGAZINES:

Cities Service Today; Chevron Focus; Chevron Marketer; Chevron World; Esso Road News; The Firing Line (Richfield); *The Lamp* (Standard Oil Company of New Jersey); *Marathon World; Mobil World; Orange Disc* (Gulf); *Our Sun* (Sunoco); *Philnews* (Phillips 66); *Selling 66* (Phillips 66); *Seventy Six* (UNOCAL); *The Soncony Standard; SOHIO; Sohio News; The Sohioan; Standard Oil Bulletin* (Standard Oil of California); *Standard Oil Scene* (Sohio); *The Texaco Dealer; and Texaco Topics.*

SOURCE CREDITS

All color photographs taken by John Margolies from 1976 to 1992 except for Stop-Agan Gas Station, page 70, Mobil Pump, page 113, and Texaco Convenience Store, page 114

All supplementary visual material from the author's collection, except as noted:

Endpapers: Compass roses from various oil company road maps.

page 1 Detail from Richfield 101 blotter, circa 1940.

page 3 Line drawing from Esso Touring Tips brochure, 1954

page 4-5 Texaco magazine advertisement, circa 1940

page 6 Comic postcard, circa 1925

page 7 Courtesy A.F. Gilmore Company

page 8 (left) Richard Miller collection

page 10 (top left) Maclean's Magazine advertisement, Peter Ledwith collection

page 10 (bottom left) Ernest Malcom collection

page 11 (center) Mike Pniewski collection

page 11 (right) Mike Pniewski collection

page 15 (top) Richard Miller collection

page 16 Courtesy Marathon Oil Company

page 18 Courtesy Phillips Petroleum Company Corporate Archive

page 19 White border postcards from the 1920s

page 20 (top right) C.A. Taubert collection

page 21 (left) Archive Photo/ J.J. Hirz

page 21 (right) Security Pacific National Bank Collection, Los Angeles Public Library

page 22 Atlantic Richfield Company Corporate Archive

page 25 (bottom center) Jim Heimann collection

page 26 Line drawing from Xerolene Motor Oil booklet, 1917

page 27 Courtesy Marathon Oil Company

page 28 Courtesy Gilbarco, Inc.

page 29 Courtesy Atlantic Richfield Company Corporate Archive

page 30 (top right) Douglas Yorke collection

page 31 (right) Courtesy Chevron Corporation

page 32 (bottom) Line drawing from booklet, "4 Wheel Fun, the 1926 Model Auto Jokes," issued by an insurance company

page 33 Courtesy Gilbarco, Inc.

page 34 Don and Newly Preziosi collection

page 37 (top center) Peter Ledwith collection

page 38-39 (bottom) Line drawing from 1934 Richfield Oil Company strip map booklet

page 40 (right) Courtesy Phillips Petroleum Company Corporate Archive

page 41 (right center) Line drawing from booklet, "4 Wheel Fun, the 1926 Model Auto Jokes," issued by an insurance company

page 42 (left) Line drawing from a 193l Sinclair road map

page 42 (top right) Douglas Yorke collection

page 44 (bottom left) Illustration from back cover of *The Socony Standard* magazine, 1926, Vol. 2, No. 5

page 44 (top right) Security Pacific National Bank Collection, Los Angeles Public Library

page 46 (top) Jim Heimann collection

page 47 (top left) Courtesy Chevron Corporation

page 47(top right) Courtesy Unocal Corporation

page 48 (top) Don and Newly Preziosi collection

page 50-51 *(top row, left to right)* Detail of illustration from 1931 Gulf road map; illustration from back cover of Union Oil Company road map, circa 1938; line drawing from Esso Touring Tips Brochure, 1954; detail of illustration from 1941 Skelly Oil Company road map; detail of illustration from Tide Water Associated Oil Company road map, circa 1948. *(middle row, left to right)* Detail of illustration from Atlantic Refining Company road map, circa 1957; detail of Richfield highway maps booklet cover, 1939; illustration from inner fold of a Sinclair road map, circa 1948; illustration from back cover of a 1940 Hi-Speed Gas road map. *(bottom row, left to right)* illustration from inner fold of a Sinclair road map, circa 1948; and illustration detail from back cover of a Union Oil Company road map, circa 1940

page 52 (top left) Tom Zimmerman collection

page 52 (top right) California State Library, Jim Lewis collection

page 53 The New Yorker

page 55 (bottom) Inner fold of 1927 Shell Motor Guide map, Douglas Yorke collection

page 56 (top left) Illustration detail from 1935 Phillips Petroleum Company road map

page 56 (middle left) Illustration detail from 1935 Phillips Petroleum Company road map, Douglas Yorke collection

page 56 (left bottom) Illustration from Pure Oil Company road map cover, circa 1935

page 57 Richard Miller collection

page 58-59 Line drawing from *The Super Service Station Magazine*, January, 1935, pp. 30-31

page 60 (bottom left) Jim Heimann collection

page 61 (right) Jim Masson collection

page 64 (top left) Auburn University Archive

page 65 Courtesy Gilbarco, Inc.

page 66-67 All line drawings from inner folds of a Deep Rock road map, circa 1950

page 67 (bottom left) Rich Musante collection

page 68 (bottom) Security Pacific National Bank Collection, Los Angeles Public Library

page 69 (top) Archive Photo

page 70 (top left) FPG International

page 70 (bottom left) Ione Wommack collection

page 71 Archive Photo

page 75 (top right) Don and Newly Preziosi collection

page 75 (bottom left) Jim Masson collection

page 76 Courtesy OXY USA

page 77 (top right) Courtesy Texaco, Inc.

page 77 (bottom left) Courtesy Texaco, Inc.

page 78 Illustration from a 1939 Shell road map

page 79 (top right) Courtesy Amoco Corporation

page 79 (bottom left) Courtesy Atlantic Richfield Corporate Archive

page 80 (bottom right) The Bettmann Archive

page 82 Courtesy OXY USA

page 84 (left) Courtesy BP America

page 84 (right) Linen postcard from World War II

page 85 The Bettmann Archive

page 88 Merchant's Photo Service, Houston

page 89 Sowell-Simon Photo

page 90 (left) Illustration from Texaco Dealers Annual Meeting magazine, 1942, page 12, Mike Pniewski collection

page 90 (right) Courtesy Mobil Corporation

page 91 Almon W. Johnston, Photographer

page 92 (top left) Courtesy OXY USA

page 92 (top center) Peter Capell collection

page 92-93 Archive Photos

page 94 Courtesy Phillips Petroleum Company Corporate Archive

page 95 (left) Courtesy Phillips Petroleum Company Corporate Archive

page 97 (bottom left) Line drawing from back cover of 1949 Standard Oil Company of Kentucky road map

page 97 (bottom right) Don and Newly Preziosi collection

page 98 Line drawing from 1961 Shell expense record pamphlet

page 100 (right) Leonard Schechter collection

page 101 Courtesy Unocal Corporation

page 102 Photographs courtesy Phillips Petroleum Company Corporate Archive

page 103 (right) Detail from cover of *The Texaco Dealer* magazine, May, 1947, Mike Pniewski collection

page 105 Comic by "Storm" from *The Texaco Dealer* magazine, May, 1947, page 16, Mike Pniewski collection

page 110 (left) Illustration from Tokheim Corporation Explorer "25" Bulletin No. 387-A brochure, 1974

page 110 (right) Illustration from Tokheim Corporation Monitor III brochure, circa 1978

page 112 (right) Courtesy A.F. Gilmore Company

page 113 (top left) Courtesy AG/ ENA

page 113 (top right and bottom) Courtesy Mobil Corporation

page 114 (top right) Anspach Grossman Portugal

page 115 Courtesy Texaco, Inc.

page 120 Don and Newly Preziosi collection

page 121 FPG International

page 122 1948-1949 Packard magazine advertisement, Jim Heimann collection

page 123 Joker illustration from a deck of Esso playing cards, circa 1960

page 125 Joker illustration from a deck of Esso playing cards, circa 1964

page 128 Esso matchbook cover illustration, circa 1960

Back flap of jacket illustration: Personalized Sunoco license plate attachment, circa 1940

Backcover: Inner fold of 1927 Shell Motor Guide map, Douglas Yorke collection

RED APPLE
Wichita, Kansas
Gas & Oil — Groceries
W. M. Reynolds, Mgr.
CONOCO
RED APPLE SERVICE STATION
RED APPLE
GROCERY
CABIN
FOR
RENT
9641

ESSO
Thanks for coming in
HURRY BACK!